Unnatural
Dykes To Watch Out For

Other books by the author:

Spawn Of Dykes To Watch Out For
Dykes To Watch Out For: The Sequel
New, Improved! Dykes To Watch Out For
More Dykes To Watch Out For
Dykes To Watch Out For

Unnatural
Dykes To Watch Out For
by Alison Bechdel

Firebrand
Books
Ithaca, New York

Alison Bechdel's cartoons appear regularly in more than fifty publications in the United States and Canada.

Book and cover design by Alison Bechdel and Debra Engstrom

Printed on acid-free paper in the United States by McNaughton & Gunn

10   9   8   7   6   5   4   3   2   1

Library of Congress Cataloging-in-Publication Data

Bechdel, Alison
    Unnatural dykes to watch out for / by Alison Bechdel.
    p.   cm.
    ISBN 1-56341-068-0. — ISBN 1-56341-067-2 (pbk.)
      1. Lesbianism—United States—Caricatures and cartoons.
2. Lesbians—United States—Caricatures and cartoons.   3. American wit and humor, Pictorial.   I. Title.
HQ75.6.U6B426   1995
306.76'63'0207—dc20   95-36092
                                                                     CIP

for Amy Rubin, of course

Thanks to the many, many people who have helped me in my work, especially the Amazon Bookstore women, Carrie Barnett and People Like Us, Helen Bechdel, Andrea Doremus, Judith Katz, Peggy Luhrs, Rachel Lurie, Patti McManamy, Amey Radcliffe and Steph Salmon at Gotham City Graphics, Alissa Oppenheimer, Sarah Van Arsdale, Jane Van Buren, the Lesbian Herstory Archives—in particular Amy Beth and Nancy Froehlich—and, as ever, Nancy Bereano. Extra special tips o' the nib to JEB (Joan E. Biren) and Kathryn Kirk, for lending me their photos of the 1981 Women's Pentagon Action.

The Mo-centric Universe

Jezanna
THE TYPE-A BOSS OF MADWIMMIN BOOKS.

Ginger
HOUSEMATE OF LOIS AND SPARROW, TEACHER, DOCTORAL CANDIDATE, AND PROCRASTINATRIX EXTRAORDINAIRE.

Mo
OUR HAPLESS HEROINE. BOOKSTORE CLERK BY DAY, CELIBATE BY NIGHT.

Lois
MO'S CO-WORKER AND CONFIDANTE, HOUSEMATE OF GINGER AND SPARROW, CONSUMMATE LOTHARIO.

Sparrow
HOUSEMATE OF LOIS AND GINGER, BATTERED WOMEN'S SHELTER WORKER, INNER-GROWTH ADDICT.

Thea
MO'S CO-WORKER AND CRUSH OBJECT.

Clarice MO'S FIRST EX-LOVER, WORKAHOLIC ATTORNEY FOR THE ENVIRON-MENTAL JUSTICE FUND, TONI'S LOVER, AND RAFAEL'S MOTHER.

Harriet MO'S MOST RECENT EX. A BUREAUCRAT FOR THE STATE, BUT A NICE PERSON NONETHELESS.

Ellen HARRIET'S CURRENT S.O., TIRELESS COMMUNITY LEADER, ACCOMPLISHED ATHLETE, AND ALL-AROUND OVERACHIEVER.

Rafael TONI AND CLARICE'S AS-YET-UNSCATHED MAN-CHILD.

Malika GINGER'S LONG-SUFFERING, LONG-DISTANCE LOVE.

Toni EMINENTLY CAPABLE MOTHER OF RAFAEL, INCREASINGLY DISCONTENTED PARTNER OF CLARICE, AND ERSTWHILE C.P.A.

June SPARROW'S NEW AND NEWLY SOBER PARAMOUR.

VOTE FOR ME

INFANT REPLAY

©1993 BY ALISON BECHDEL

171

Panel 1:
MALIKA, I'M GONNA **SMASH** THAT FUCKING CAMCORDER!

YEAH, THIS IS RIGHT BEFORE THE BABY CROWNS.

SHE'S GETTING REALLY CLOSE NOW!

FONY

Panel 2:
THERE'S THE HEAD! JEEZ, IT'S ALMOST AS INTENSE ON TV AS IN REAL LIFE!

LOOK HOW BEAUTIFUL TONI IS, POISED ON THE BRINK OF THIS MIRACULOUS RITE OF PASSAGE!

UNNGH!

Panel 3:
OH MY GOD!

WHAT AN INCREDIBLE SHOT!

I STILL CAN'T BELIEVE IT.

Panel 4:
MEANWHILE, OVER AT THE BIRTHING CENTER... OH, WOW... IT FEELS WEIRD! I CAN'T BELIEVE THIS IS REALLY GONNA WORK.. ...AY!

MAKE SURE YOU'RE DEEP IN. HE NEEDS TO LATCH ONTO YOUR BREAST, NOT JUST THE NIPPLE. THERE, HE'S SUCKING!

9

revelations
© 1993 BY ALISON BECHDEL
172
ONE RAINY MORNING AT MADWIMMIN BOOKS . . .
THEA, YOU SHOULDN'T DRINK COFFEE WHILE YOU'RE ON THE COMPUTER. WHAT IF IT SPILLS?
RELAX, MO. I'M VERY CAREFUL.
SHEESH! WHAT'S UP HER BUTT? SHE'S BEEN ACTING REALLY WEIRD TOWARD ME LATELY.
OKAY, YOU MIGHT AS WELL KNOW. THE OTHER DAY, SHE OVERHEARD YOU TELLING ME HOW PUPPYLIKE YOU FIND HER CRUSH ON YOU.
FEMINIST BOOKSTORE SCHMOOZE
SHIT! SHE MUST FEEL AWFUL! I'D BETTER TALK TO HER.
OFFICE
OH, JEEZ. I HATE LESBIAN HONESTY. LOOK, JUST DON'T TELL HER I TOLD YOU SHE HEARD WHAT YOU TOLD ME.
CLARICE! WHAT ARE YOU DOING HERE WITH A TWO-DAY-OLD KID AT HOME? STIR-CRAZY ALREADY?
I NEED SOME BOOKS ABOUT BABIES, FAST.
WHAT'S WRONG, CLARICE?

11

a rock and a hard place
173
©1993 BY ALISON BECHDEL
HEY, CLARICE! I THOUGHT I'D DROP IN AND RELIEVE THE BOREDOM AND ISOLATION OF YOUR LIMITED LITTLE NUCLEAR FAMILY CIRCLE. HELLO, RAFAEL!
SAY HELLO TO AUNT MO! TELL HER SHE JUST MISSED YOUR FEEDING AND YOUR DIAPER CHANGE AND YOUR BURP!
BUT MAYBE YOU'RE BEYOND HELP.
AND WHAT A WORLD-CLASS BURP IT WAS, MY LITTLE SUGARTOES!
HI, TONI! HOW'RE THEY HANGING?
OH, GOD. MY NIPPLES ARE CRACKED, I'M CONSTANTLY LEAKING, HE EATS EVERY TWO HOURS 'ROUND THE CLOCK... I FEEL LIKE A FUCKING HOLSTEIN.
HONEY, NO MORE SWEARING, REMEMBER?
CHIPS
LA LECHE
MO, DID YOU SEE OUR BIRTH ANNOUNCEMENT IN THE LATEST TRIBUNE?
NOT YET. BUT ISN'T THIS PIECE ABOUT THE NATIONAL GAY AND LESBIAN TASK FORCE INTERESTING?
10% TRIBUNE
NGLTF HEAD QUITS
CHIPS

THE HIGH-POWERED EXECUTIVE DIRECTOR RESIGNS AFTER SIX MONTHS, IN A CLASH OVER STRATEGIES TO EXPAND THE ORGANIZATION. DON'T YOU LOVE THIS STUFF?

SOUNDS LIKE SHE WANTED TO TURN THE GRASSROOTS ACTIVIST-BASED TASK FORCE INTO A MORE CORPORATE, MAINSTREAM POLITICAL POWER, LIKE THE HUMAN RIGHTS CHAMPAGNE FUND.

IT'S AN INTERESTING DILEMMA, THOUGH. HOW DOES A NONPROFIT GAIN ENOUGH BUCKS AND INFLUENCE TO TAKE ON THE RELIGIOUS RIGHT, YET NOT LOSE THE PULSE OF THE QUEER ON THE STREET?

HEY, CHECK OUT THIS FACE HE MAKES WHEN HE HAS GAS!

READ OUR ANNOUNCEMENT, MO. IT'S ON PAGE 10.

OKAY, OKAY! **HEY!** ISN'T THIS HARRIET'S NEW GIRLFRIEND?!

WHIMPER...

YEAH! SHE'S RUNNING AGAINST SOME TRADITIONAL VALUES COALITION TYPE TO REPRESENT OUR WARD ON THE CITY COUNCIL!

VOTE! ELLEN TUFEL

"HATE IS NOT A FAMILY VALUE."

CITY COUNCIL 3RD WARD

COMMUNITY

OH, THAT'S JUST **GREAT**. WHO AM I GONNA **VOTE** FOR?

WAAA!

13

hot stuff

©1993 BY ALISON BECHDEL

It's Saturday evening...

OUCH! LOOKS LIKE YOU CLOSED YOUR MOUTH TOO CLOSE TO THE FLAME.

NO KIDDING.

WHAT?

174

LOIS BURNT HER LIP EATING FIRE WITH THE LESBIAN AVENGERS.

IT WAS SO COOL! YOU SHOULDA BEEN THERE! Y'KNOW DICK LILLY, THE TRADITIONAL VALUES COALITION GUY WHO'S RUNNING FOR CITY COUNCIL?

WE PICKETED HIS PANCAKE BREAKFAST FUND-RAISER DRESSED UP LIKE GIANT FLAMING CRÊPES SUZETTES!

Y'KNOW, THAT REMINDS ME OF ONE TIME BEFORE I GOT SOBER WHEN A BUDDY LIT MY APRICOT BRANDY ON FIRE AND SINGED ALL MY EYELASHES...

COME ON, JUNE, OR WE'LL MISS OUR MEETING.

Meanwhile, over at Madwimmin Books...

I'M SORRY, WE'RE CLOSING.

OH... I JUST WANTED TO DROP OFF THIS CAMPAIGN POSTER FOR ELLEN TUFEL. COULD YOU PUT IT UP ON YOUR BULLETIN BOARD?

VOTE! ELLEN TUFEL CITY COUNCIL "HATE IS NOT A FAMILY VALUE"

14

GOT A BIG NIGHT PLANNED, MO?

OH, YEAH! I HAVE TO RUSH—LAST LOAD'S GOTTA BE IN BY 7:30 AT DUDS 'N SUDS! WHAT ABOUT YOU AND MAXINE? A QUIET EVENING AT HOME, ACTING OUT SCENES FROM "CLAIRE OF THE MOON?"

OKAY, THAT'S IT. WE HAVE TO TALK. YOU'VE BEEN MAKING LITTLE DIGS AT ME ALL WEEK. IF THIS IS BECAUSE YOU'RE FEELING HURT THAT I DON'T HAVE A CRUSH BACK ON YOU, ALL I CAN SAY IS I'M SORRY, AND I'M FLATTERED, BUT...

BUT YOU JUST DON'T THINK OF ME THAT WAY, AND BESIDES, YOU'RE IN A RELATIONSHIP ALREADY, AND YOU HOPE WE CAN STILL BE FRIENDS.

WELL... YEAH.

OH, OKAY! SO THAT MUST HAVE BEEN MAXINE YOU WERE SUGGESTIVELY REFERRING TO AS A "BABE" WITH LOIS THE OTHER DAY. I THOUGHT IT WAS ME, BUT THE ACOUSTICS IN HERE AREN'T THE GREATEST.

JEEZIZ! WHAT ARE YOU DOING, SLINKING AROUND SPYING ON PEOPLE?

HAH! I KNEW IT!

OKAY. SO MAYBE I AM A LITTLE BIT ATTRACTED TO YOU. BUT IT DOESN'T MATTER BECAUSE ABSOLUTELY NOTHING'S GOING TO HAPPEN. GOT IT?

WOW! I NEVER SAW YOU BLUSH BEFORE! IT'S SO, UM... CUTE.

HI, SWEETIE! HI, MO! THEA, I'M DOUBLE-PARKED OUT FRONT. LOOKS LIKE YOU HAD A BIG DAY! THE WINDOWS ARE ALL STEAMED UP!

15

ADVICE & DISSENT

(175)

©1993 BY ALISON BECHDEL

YOU TOLD HER YOU WERE ATTRACTED TO HER BUT YOU'RE NOT GONNA HAVE AN AFFAIR? I DON'T GET IT.

LOIS, HAVEN'T YOU EVER BEEN ATTRACTED TO A PERSON AND NOT ACTED ON IT?

NO. ALTHOUGH I HAVE ACTED ON IT WITH PEOPLE I WASN'T PARTICULAR-LY ATTRACTED TO.

HOW NICE FOR YOU. LISTEN, MAXINE AND I ARE COMMITTED TO A MONOGAMOUS RELATIONSHIP, BUT WE'VE AGREED IT'S HEALTHY TO ACKNOWLEDGE OUR FEELINGS FOR OTHER WOMEN.

SO WHY NOT ACKNOWLEDGE THEM ALL THE WAY? ISN'T THAT EVEN HEALTHIER? MO HASN'T **GOTTEN ANY** IN OVER A YEAR! IMAGINE HOW HOT SHE'D BE!

COULD YOU PLEASE KEEP YOUR VOICE DOWN? IT WAS YOUR BIG MOUTH THAT STARTED THIS WHOLE THING IN THE FIRST PLACE!

CHERRY GROVE, FLAMING ISLAND

MADONNA-TRAUMA ESSAYS ON BASICALLY NOTHING

UH, THEA.. SOME-ONE NEEDS INFORMA-TION ABOUT A COM-PACT DISC.

OVER A YEAR!

OKAY. THANKS, MO.

LOIS, DID YOU FEEL THAT? COULD YOU SENSE THE **ELECTRICITY** BETWEEN US? I CAN'T STAND IT!

16

17

18

19

...PLANNING FOR THE FUTURE,...

EXPLORING INTIMACY...

AND BONDING AROUND LIFE'S DIFFICULTIES.

A KISS is just A KISS

178

© 1993 BY ALISON BECHDEL

MMM. JEZANNA'S DOUBLE CHOCO- LATE RASPBERRY ESPRESSO NEW YEAR'S CHEESECAKE IS **ORGASMIC.**

UH... YEAH, IT IS. CAN I GET YOU ANOTHER PIECE?

ENJOYING THE PARTY, GIRLS? THEA, I'M **SO** SORRY MAXINE COULDN'T MAKE IT!

THANKS, JEZ. SHE'S GOT THE FLU.

LOIS, THE BOBBSEY TWINS OVER THERE ARE MAKING ME NERVOUS. THEIR LITTLE CRUSH WAS CUTE FOR A WHILE, BUT I CAN'T AFFORD TO HAVE TWO OF MY EMPLOYEES INVOLVED IN SOME SORDID SEXUAL SOAP OPERA.

RELAX. IT'S NOT A REAL ATTRACTION. IF THEA WAS ACTUALLY AVAILABLE, THEY WOULDN'T KNOW WHAT TO DO WITH EACH OTHER.

HUNH. LOOKS TO ME LIKE THEY'D HAVE A PRETTY GOOD IDEA.

OKAY. I'LL TAKE CARE OF IT. IT'S TIME MO GOT ON WITH HER LIFE, ANYWAY.

HEY! GREAT PARTY, HUH?

WHAT I LOVE BEST ABOUT NEW YEAR'S EVE IS THAT LITTLE WINDOW OF SEXUAL LAWLESSNESS AT MIDNIGHT WHEN YOU GET TO KISS EVERYONE. KIND OF LIKE GROWN-UP SPIN-THE-BOTTLE.

Y'KNOW, I'VE ALWAYS REGRETTED THAT I NEVER GOT TO PLAY SPIN-THE-BOTTLE WITH OTHER LITTLE DYKES WHEN I WAS A KID, INSTEAD OF BOYS.

I NEVER GOT TO PLAY SPIN THE BOTTLE WITH ANYONE.

FIVE... FOUR... THREE ...TWO... ONE..

HAPPY NEW YEAR!

SLURP!

SMACK!

IN THE WEE HOURS OF JANUARY FIRST...

JEEZ. I HOPE I DIDN'T CATCH ANY OF MAXINE'S **FLU** GERMS FROM THEA.

BELIEVE ME, YOU'RE GONNA BE JUST FINE.

on her back

© 1994 BY ALISON BECHDEL

(180)

ONE AFTERNOON AMID THE BUSTLE AND COMMERCE OF OUR FAVORITE FEMINIST BOOK EMPORIUM...

...AND WHEN YOU'RE DONE UNPACKING THOSE, CHECK THEM OFF ON THE PURCHASE ORDER BEFORE YOU...

OW!

BOOKS

SPINSTER'S INK

SEX, ART, AMERICAN CULTURE AND ME

GIRL, HOW MANY TIMES HAVE I TOLD YOU TO BEND YOUR KNEES WHEN YOU LIFT?

OH, *#@◑!

BY CAMILLE PAGLIA 50 COPIES

DAMN. CAN YOU MOVE?

DON'T TOUCH ME!

DO YOU HAVE A CHIROPRACTOR, MO?

LOOKS LIKE A JOB FOR DR. NAVARRO.

I'LL CALL HER.

UNH!

NEED A RIDE TO HER OFFICE, MO?

SPARROW SWEARS BY THIS CHIROPRACTOR. SAYS SHE'S A GODDESS IN HUMAN FORM. WHOA! WHEN ARE THEY GONNA FILL THESE POTHOLES?

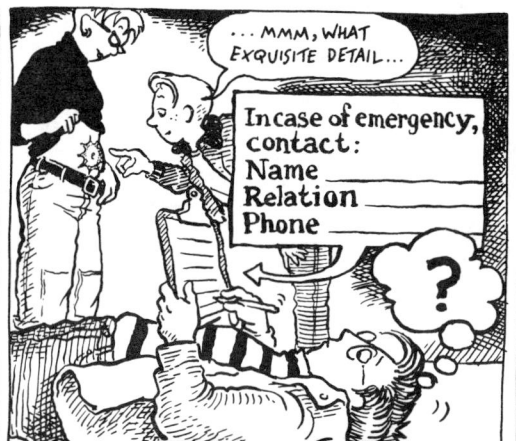

BROKEN, ALONE, AND REFERRED TO IN THE THIRD PERSON WHILE STILL PRESENT... CAN OUR HEROINE POSSIBLY SINK ANY LOWER? DON'T MISS THE NEXT TAUT, WRENCHING EPISODE!

LOYALTY

© 1994 BY ALISON BECHDEL

182

30

31

LET GO AND LET MO

© 1994 BY ALISON BECHDEL

(183)

LO-IS! COME DOWN HERE PLEASE!

UM.. COULD YOU EXCUSE ME A MINUTE, BABE?

SHEESH! WHAT DO YOU WANT, SPARROW?!

WHAT IS **THIS** DOING IN THE REFRIGERATOR?

WOW! A BOTTLE OF DRECK'S DARK! THAT WAS MY FAVORITE!

SONYA BROUGHT IT OVER TO HAVE WITH DINNER LATER. WHY?

I USED TO LOVE TO KNOCK BACK TWO OR THREE OF THESE WHILE I WAS COOKING. IT WAS THE SECRET INGREDIENT IN MY STIR-FRY! I HAVEN'T BEEN ABLE TO GET THE FLAVOR RIGHT SINCE.

LOIS, I THOUGHT WE AGREED NOT TO BRING ALCOHOL INTO THE HOUSE!

OH, YEAH. I GUESS I WASN'T THINKING. I MEAN, IT'S JUST A BOTTLE OF BEER.

AH, THAT DARK AMBER LIQUID...THE HEAVY, MALTY FEEL AS I SWALLOWED... THE BITTER TASTE OF HOPS LEFT ON MY TONGUE....THE SOOTHING BUZZ SETTING IN JUST BEHIND MY CHEEKBONES...

JUNE, **GIVE** ME THAT!

33

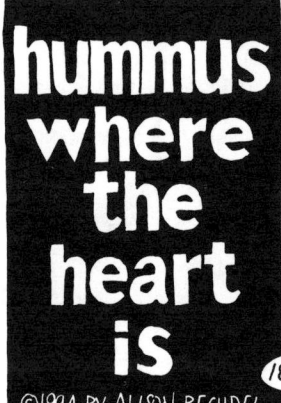

hummus where the heart is

184

©1994 BY ALISON BECHDEL

GINGER IS EXPECTED HOME IMMINENTLY FROM THE BLACK GAY AND LESBIAN LEADERSHIP FORUM CONFERENCE, AND MO HAS DROPPED BY FOR DINNER.

OKAY. I'M ALL DONE WITH MY FAMOUS HUMMUS À LA MO. AS SOON AS GINGER GETS HERE, WE CAN EAT.

INSTANT! JUST ADD H₂O!

WHOA! CAN YOU BELIEVE ALL THESE SCI-FI RADIATION TESTS THE GOVERNMENT DID IN THE 40'S AND 50'S? DOCTORS DIDN'T EVEN **TELL** PEOPLE THEY WERE INJECTING THEM WITH PLUTONIUM!

YEAH. HOW CONVENIENT NO ONE'S ADMITTING IT UNTIL 50 YEARS AFTER THE FACT. MAYBE IN 2044, THEY'LL CONFESS TO ALL THE STUFF THEY'RE DOING **NOW**.

F.D.A. SEZ: MILK HORMONES ARE GOOD FOR YOU

The Distress

WHINE.

LIKE HOW THE ARMY FORCED SOLDIERS IN THE GULF WAR TO TAKE ALL KINDS OF EXPERIMENTAL ANTI-BOTULISM AND ANTI-NERVE GAS DRUGS. NOW THEY'VE GOT BIZARRE ILLNESSES, THEIR BABIES ARE DEFORMED, AND THE DEPARTMENT OF DEFENSE DOESN'T SEE A CONNECTION.

NO SHIT!

LOIS, YOU ARE SO NAIVE!

The Distress

ARF!

HELLO! I'M BACK! DIGGER! COME TO MAMA, YOU BIG WOLF-GIRL!

GINGER!

WELCOME HOME!

HOW WAS THE CONFERENCE?

OH, IT WAS GREAT! THE GRASSROOTS ORGANIZING WORKSHOP REALLY GOT ME ALL CHARGED UP! AND I GOT ME'SHELL NDEGEOCELLO'S AUTOGRAPH AFTER SHE PERFORMED SATURDAY.

the AWAKEN-ING

(185)

© 1994 BY ALISON BECHDEL

ANYA, I'VE BEEN IN THERAPY WITH YOU FOR **FOUR YEARS** NOW, AND IT'S BEEN **TWO** SINCE HARRIET LEFT ME! WHEN AM I GONNA COME OUT OF THIS **SLUMP?**

I THOUGHT THINGS WERE TURNING AROUND WHEN THEA STARTED FLIRTING WITH ME, BUT THAT WAS JUST A DEAD END. I MEAN, WHAT DID I EXPECT? SHE AND MAXINE OWN A FUCKING **CONDO** TOGETHER.

THEN THIS BACK TROUBLE! I WAKE UP ALL STIFF EVERY MORNING, ALONE IN MY BED. I'M NOT GETTING ANY YOUNGER, YOU KNOW...

THAT'S ENOUGH, MO. I CAN'T STAND ONE MORE SYLLABLE OF YOUR SELF-INDULGENT SNIVELLING!

YOU'RE OBVIOUSLY NOT INTER-ESTED IN CHANGING YOUR LIFE, SO STOP WASTING MY VALUABLE TIME AND GET OUT OF THIS OFFICE IMMEDIATELY.

NOW! I'LL MAIL YOU THE BILL!

B-BUT I...

POOF!

36

SORRY TO WAKE YOU, MO. I'M ALL DONE WITH THE ULTRA-SOUND. NOW I'M GOING TO DO AN ADJUSTMENT.

SCHXX!

!

Shortly...

HOW'RE YOU FEELING, MO?

Y'KNOW, I ACTUALLY FEEL **GREAT!** HOW 'BOUT THAT?

DR. ANGELA NAVARRO CHIROPRACT

IT'S LIKE I'M A NEW PERSON! JEEZ, I'VE GOTTA GET OFF MY BUTT! SEIZE THE DAY! JOIN THE **Y!** BECOME A VEGAN! READ THE FRENCH FEMINISTS!

KA LUNK

I'LL BABYSIT RAFAEL SO CLARICE AND TONI CAN GO OUT MORE. AND LOIS HAS BEEN BUGGING ME TO COME TO A LESBIAN AVENGERS MEETING FOR MONTHS. WHAT AM I WAITING FOR? I'M SURE THEY COULD BENEFIT FROM MY INSIGHTS!

I'LL TAKE THAT COMPUTER CLASS JEZ WAS HINTING ABOUT AT WORK.... AND I'LL VOLUNTEER TO ORGANIZE READINGS BY LOCAL WRITERS AT THE BOOKSTORE. HECK, I'LL START WRITING AGAIN **MYSELF!**

*W*HAT HAS BECOME OF MO'S OLD, ENDEARING **MALAISE?** IS THIS GROTESQUE ZEST FOR LIFE MERELY A TEMPORARY SIDE-EFFECT, OR HAS DR. NAVARRO CREATED A **MONSTER** ?

WEIGHTY MATTERS

© 1994 BY ALISON BECHDEL

186

STRANGELY ENERGIZED BY HER RECENT CHIROPRACTIC ADJUSTMENT, OUR HEROINE UNDERTAKES AN AMBITIOUS REGIMEN OF SELF-IMPROVEMENT.

...NINE...**TEN!** OKAY, YOU'RE ALL DONE, MO! THAT'S THE LAST MACHINE ON THE CIRCUIT. NOT BAD FOR YOUR FIRST DAY. A FEW MONTHS WORKING OUT LIKE THAT, AND YOU'LL BE IN DECENT SHAPE!

GUT BUSTER

ARR!

STAFF

UNH.

WOMEN'S LOCKER ROOM

HARRIET?!

MO! WHAT ARE **YOU** DOING HERE?!

I JUST JOINED! I'M TURNING OVER A NEW LEAF, HARRIET! I'M GETTING A LOT MORE ACTIVE AND INVOLVED IN THE COMMU...

MO! NICE TO SEE YOU HERE! LOOKIN' GOOD!

UM... HI, ELLEN.

HARRIET, WE'RE GOING OUT FOR DINNER TONIGHT, RIGHT? I'LL BE DONE WITH MY GAME AT EIGHT.

GREAT. I'LL MEET YOU IN THE SAUNA.

SO HARRIET, WHAT ARE **YOU** DOING HERE? WHEN WE WERE TOGETHER, YOU ALWAYS SAID EXERCISE WAS AN ANTI-FEMINIST PLOT TO MAKE WOMEN LOSE WEIGHT AND DISAPPEAR.

I KNOW. BUT I'VE ALWAYS LIKED SWIMMING. AND THIS IS THE ONLY TIME I GET TO SEE ELLEN LATELY, SHE'S SO BUSY.

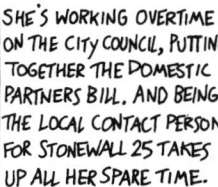

SHE'S WORKING OVERTIME ON THE CITY COUNCIL, PUTTING TOGETHER THE DOMESTIC PARTNERS BILL. AND BEING THE LOCAL CONTACT PERSON FOR STONEWALL 25 TAKES UP ALL HER SPARE TIME.

PLUS SHE'S IN TRAINING FOR THE GAY GAMES. SHE AND HER RACQUETBALL PARTNER PLAY FOUR TIMES A WEEK.

REALLY.

SO WHAT'S THIS NEW LEAF YOU'RE TURNING OVER?

OH. UH... NEVER MIND. BUT SPEAKING OF STONE-WALL 25, DON'T YOU THINK THIS HUGE, SLICK PARTY THEY'RE THROWING BETRAYS THE REVOLUTIONARY SPIRIT OF THE '69 RIOT JUST A **TAD?** I'M SURE THE CHRISTIAN RIGHT IS JUST THRILLED WE'LL BE SPENDING A ZILLION BUCKS VACATIONING IN NEW YORK INSTEAD OF ON FIGHTING ALL THE ANTI-GAY INITIATIVES COMING UP THIS YEAR.

YOU SHOULD TELL ELLEN THAT.

MAYBE AFTER I BULK UP A LITTLE.

THE CAPTIVE

187

© 1994 BY ALISON BECHDEL

HE'S ALL READY FOR BED. JUST PUT HIM IN HIS CRIB IN HALF AN HOUR OR SO. ARE YOU SURE YOU'LL BE OKAY, MO?

TONI, I KNOW WHAT I'M DOING! I'M A RESPONSIBLE ADULT! THE KID'LL STILL BE ALIVE WHEN YOU GET BACK. NOW GO!

OKAY, RAFAEL. WHAT'LL WE DO UNTIL BED-TIME?

SHRIEK!

HEY, IT'S OKAY! THEY DIDN'T REALLY ABANDON YOU! THEY JUST LEFT YOU WITH YOUR AUNT MO FOR A COUPLE HOURS. I'M GREAT WITH KIDS!

WAIL!

WAAAAAAAAAA

the best policy

© 1994 BY ALISON BECHDEL

(188)

MALIKA'S COMING FOR THE WEEKEND. I WAS THINKING MAYBE YOU AND I SHOULD CLEAR OUT TONIGHT SO SHE AND GINGER CAN HAVE SOME TIME ALONE.

HOW THOUGHTFUL, IF UNCHARACTERISTIC OF YOU, LOIS. SO, I GUESS IF MALIKA'S FLYING IN ALL THE WAY FROM SAN FRANCISCO, SHE MUST HAVE FORGIVEN GINGER'S LITTLE CONFERENCE TRYST.

UH... GINGER DECIDED IT WASN'T THE SORT OF THING SHE COULD TELL HER OVER THE PHONE.

OH MY GOD! POOR MALIKA! Y'KNOW, I THINK I'LL CLEAR OUT FOR THE WHOLE WEEKEND.

ME TOO. I'LL BE AT SONYA'S. NORMALLY I AVOID WEEKEND-LONG DATES -- THERE'S SOMETHING SO SORDIDLY DOMESTIC ABOUT WAKING UP TWO DAYS IN A ROW WITH THE SAME PERSON -- BUT IN THIS CASE, I'M MAKING AN EXCEPTION.

CLIK!

HI, MALIKA! YOU LOOK GREAT! HOW WAS YOUR FLIGHT?

RIF!

A TIP O' THE NIB TO RACHEL LURIE!

GOTTA RUN!

CIAO!

SLAM!

NOW ALL THREE OF YOU ARE ACTING FISHY. WHAT'S GOING ON? DID YOU LEAVE ONE OF OUR "PERSONAL" VIDEOTAPES IN THE VCR AGAIN?

MEANWHILE, CLARICE IS HOME FROM THE SALT MINES.

HEY, A PACKAGE FROM YOUR PARENTS! WHY HAVEN'T YOU OPENED IT?

I'M AFRAID IT'S A BOMB.

AH PEE BAH

MAYBE IT'S A BABY PRESENT. YOU HAVEN'T HEARD FROM THEM SINCE RAFFI WAS BORN. THEIR GUILT REFLEXES MUST FINALLY BE KICKING IN. LET'S OPEN IT!

AJA!

TOLD YOU IT WAS A BOMB.

"THANK YOU FOR THE SNAPSHOTS. HE LOOKS SO MUCH LIKE YOUR TÍO HECTOR. I JUST PRAY YOU'VE TAKEN HIM TO BE BAPTIZED, AND THAT IT'S NOT TOO LATE FOR YOU TO FIND A HUSBAND. A CHILD NEEDS TWO PARENTS, AND A BOY ESPECIALLY NEEDS A FATHER."

TONI...

I KNOW, I KNOW. I HAVE TO DO IT. AFTER ALL, WHAT KIND OF AN EXAMPLE AM I SETTING RAFAEL IF I CAN'T TELL MY OWN PARENTS I'M A LESBIAN?

BELIEVE ME, HON. TELLING THEM THE TRUTH CAN ULTIMATELY ONLY IMPROVE YOUR RELATIONSHIP.

AM I **MAD** AT YOU? FOR DIDDLING SOME BIMBO? OH, GIRL. WHEN I GET MAD, YOU WON'T HAVE TO ASK. I'M JUST WARMING UP. I GOTTA **PACE** MYSELF IF I WANT TO MAKE YOU **SUFFER** WITHOUT **PAUSE** FOR THE REMAINDER OF YOUR BORN DAYS.

43

brunette ambition

© 1994 BY ALISON BECHDEL

(189)

HI, I'M MIKO. I SAW THE NOTICE ABOUT THE "MADWIM-MIN READ" SERIES FOR LOCAL LESBIAN WRITERS, AND I WANTED TO DROP OFF SOME OF MY WORK.

OH, GREAT! YOU'RE THE THIRD PERSON TO SUBMIT STUFF! I THINK WE'RE GONNA HAVE SOME EXCITING READINGS. LET ME LOOK THIS OVER, AND THEN I'LL CALL YOU ABOUT A DATE.

HEY, GIRL! I DIDN'T KNOW YOU WERE A WRITER!

HI, LOIS! YEAH, I'VE BEEN PUBLISHED IN A FEW JOURNALS, AND I JUST SENT MY FIRST MANUSCRIPT OUT. IT'S A COLLECTION OF STORIES ABOUT MY CLIENTS.

UH... REALLY!

DON'T WORRY. I CHANGED YOUR NAME AND MADE YOU A BRUNETTE.

COOL. LISTEN, I HAVE TO SCHEDULE A HAIRCUT BEFORE STONEWALL 25.

SURE. I'M ON MY WAY TO THE SALON NOW. CALL ME AND WE'LL SET SOME-THING UP.

NICE 'DO!

SHEESH, LOIS. NEW CLOTHES, A HAIRCUT... AS IF YOU'RE NOT ALREADY DROPPING **ENOUGH** MONEY JUST TRAVELING TO THAT OVERHYPED SHINDIG.

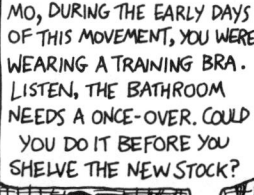

unminced words

© 1994 BY ALISON BECHDEL

190

FFF BO N-DWEE YA GAH!

REALLY! I HAD NO IDEA!

ISN'T HIS BABBLING EXPRESSIVE? IT'S LIKE HE'S ACTUALLY SAYING SOMETHING!

WATCH OUT. HE MIGHT GET ELECTED TO PUBLIC OFFICE.

AND WHAT'S THE MATTER WITH PUBLIC OFFICE, HARRIET?

CLINTON GRANTS MOST FAVORED NATION STATUS TO CHINA

SELT-ZA

I DIDN'T MEAN YOU AND THE CITY COUNCIL, ELLEN. I'M JUST DEPRESSED ABOUT THE STATE OF AMERICAN POLITICS IN GENERAL.

YEAH. CLINTON'S TURNING OUT TO BE A REAL DISAPPOINTMENT.

HEY, I'D RATHER BE DISAPPOINTED THAN FEARFUL FOR MY LIFE, LIKE I WAS UNDER REAGAN AND BUSH. WHAT GETS ME IS THE WAY THESE OBSESSIVE CONSERVATIVES KEEP TRYING TO TRIP CLINTON UP. I MEAN, LET THE GUY DO HIS JOB!

I THINK THEIR LITTLE TRICKS ARE BACKFIRING. TO MOST PEOPLE, IT'S OBVIOUS THAT THE WHITEWATER ALLEGATIONS AND THE SEXUAL HARASSMENT SUIT ARE POLITICALLY MOTIVATED. AND EVERYONE ELSE IS TOO JADED TO CARE IF BILL FUCKS HIS CAT.

FUCKS!

CLINTON SIGNS ABORTION ACCESS LAW

DO YOU WANT THE HONOR OF RECORDING THAT UNDER "BABY'S FIRST WORD," OR SHALL I?

MEANWHILE, MALIKA'S VISIT DRAWS TO A CLOSE...

HERE'S A NEWS FLASH. "A RECENT STUDY SHOWS AFRICAN AMERICAN GAY MEN AND WOMEN HAVE SUBSTANTIALLY HIGHER LEVELS OF CHRONIC STRESS THAN HETEROSEXUAL BLACKS AND WHITES, AND LESBIAN AFRICAN AMERICANS SUFFER FROM MORE STRESS THAN THEIR GAY COUNTERPARTS."

A TIP O' THE NIB TO BARBARA SMITH

I GUESS PEOPLE CAN GRASP THE CONCEPT BETTER IF YOU CALL IT 'STRESS' INSTEAD OF 'OPPRESSION.'

GINGER, WILL YOU STOP CHANGING THE SUBJECT? MY FLIGHT'S LEAVING SOON AND I WANT TO KNOW: ARE YOU COMMITTED TO THIS RELATIONSHIP OR NOT?

MALIKA, THAT WOMAN MEANT **NOTHING** TO ME, OKAY? IT WAS A STUPID LITTLE FLING, AND I'M SORRY!

FINE! FORGET ABOUT HER! WHAT I'M TRYING TO SAY IS, I LOVE YOU AND I WANT US TO LIVE TOGETHER. IF YOU DON'T FEEL THE SAME, I'VE GOTTA RETHINK MY PLANS.

L-LIVE TOGETHER? JEEZ, BABE... YOU KNOW HOW IMPORTANT MY WORK IS TO ME RIGHT NOW. I'M TOTALLY WRAPPED UP IN MY DISSERTATION! COULDN'T WE TALK ABOUT THIS LATER?

WE DON'T HAVE TO. THAT'S ALL I NEEDED TO HEAR.

SWEETIE, ALL I MEANT WAS, I CAN'T MOVE TO SAN FRANCISCO BECAUSE OF SCHOOL. AND YOU CAN'T MOVE HERE BECAUSE, UM, LIKE, THERE'S NO ROOM FOR ANY OF YOUR STUFF!

THAT'S FOR DAMN SURE. WILL DRIVING ME TO THE AIRPORT BE TOO MUCH **STRESS** FOR YOU OR SHOULD I TAKE THE BUS?

Ginger snaps

© 1994 BY ALISON BECHDEL

Mo VISITS OUR HARRIED HOUSEMATES ON THE EVE OF THEIR JOURNEY TO THE GAY GAMES AND STONEWALL 25.

191

...THEN SHE FLEW BACK TO FRISCO AND TOLD ME NOT TO BOTHER CALLING UNTIL I KNEW WHAT I WANTED.

JEEZ!

RATTLE RATTLE

OKAY, SO YOU JUST FILL THE BOWL TO THE TOP WITH CHOW ONCE A DAY AFTER THE EVENING WALK.

GOT IT. I'LL TAKE GOOD CARE OF HER. SO GINGER, WHAT **DO** YOU WANT?

IF I KNEW THAT, I WOULDN'T HAVE A **PROBLEM**, WOULD I?

THE WASHER'S ALL YOURS, GINGER. MO, COME UP-STAIRS AND HELP ME PACK.

SNARF

WHAT'S YOUR GOAL THIS TIME? YOU GONNA TRY AND KISS A WOMAN FROM EVERY COMPETING COUN-TRY AT THE GAMES?

NAH. I'M TAKING A MORE THEMATIC APPROACH TO THIS EVENT. I HOPE TO **GROPE** AN ATHLETE FROM EACH SPORT...

AND GO FOR THE GOLD WITH A MARATHON RUNNER, A WATERPOLO PLAYER, A DIVER, AND A WRESTLER.

I GUESS SONYA'S NOT GOING WITH YOU THEN.

48

OH, SHE'S COMING! SHE'S COVERING BODY BUILDERS, CYCLISTS, AND IN-LINE SKATERS. SHE HAS A THIGH THING.

HEY, HOW DO WE LOOK?

WHOA! I DIDN'T KNOW YOU TWO WERE INTO CROSS-DRESSING! JUNE, YOU MAKE A SURPRISINGLY HOT FEMME.

DON'T I? ADAM LENT ME THE DRESS, AND I LENT MY TUX TO SPARROW.

WHAT'S THE OCCASION?

THE ASIAN LESBIAN NETWORK GALA IN NEW YORK. WILL WE BE ABLE TO HANG THIS STUFF UP IN YOUR CAR SO IT DOESN'T WRINKLE, LOIS?

WITH FIVE OF US CRAMMED IN THAT DECREPIT BUG? BRING AN IRON.

SKRITCH

GINGER, I HOPE YOU LOSE THE ATTITUDE BEFORE IT'S TIME TO GO. WHAT'S THE PROBLEM? MALIKA'S OFF YOUR BACK, AND SOON YOU'LL BE CRUISING THOUSANDS OF PRIME PHYSICAL SPECIMENS FROM ALL OVER THE GLOBE!

LOIS, GIVE HER A LITTLE SUPPORT! SHE'S SUFFERING FROM A DEEP, INTERNAL CONFLICT BETWEEN HER INTENSE **LONGING** FOR INTIMACY, AND THE BELIEF THAT SHE'S BASICALLY **UNWORTHY** OF IT.

SPARROW?

SHOVE IT UP YOUR CUMMERBUND.

IT'S HARD TO SEE SOMEONE SO OUT OF TOUCH WITH HER TRUE FEELINGS. MAYBE WE CAN GET HER TO TALK ABOUT IT DURING THE DRIVE TOMORROW.

OH, I'D LIKE THAT. LET'S ALL EAT LOTS OF BEANS FOR BREAKFAST, TOO.

49

Lost in Paradise

©1994 BY ALISON BECHDEL

(192)

AFTER SPENDING THE DAY APART IN ORDER TO ACHIEVE A WIDER SAMPLING OF NEW YORK CITY'S DIZZYING **GLUT** OF QUEER CULTURAL AND ATHLETIC EVENTS, GINGER, LOIS, SPARROW AND JUNE HAVE PLANNED TO **RENDEZVOUS** AT THE **INTERNATIONAL DYKE MARCH**.

HUH... MAYBE WE SHOULDA PICKED A PARTICULAR CORNER.

HEY, **MATTIE!**

DAMNED LESBIANS

REMEMBER ME? THE BGLLF CONFERENCE? WE, UM... ORDERED **ROOM SERVICE** TOGETHER!

OH, ER... HI. GINGER, RIGHT? THIS IS MY LOVER, PRISCILLA.

GINGER, HUH? I HOPE YOU STAYED AWAY FROM THE SEAFOOD.

MAMA WAS A FEMME

TEAM ATLANTA WRESTLING

*M*EANWHILE, SPARROW GROWS ANXIOUS...

WHERE **ARE** THOSE GIRLS? THE MARCH IS STARTING!

EXCUSE ME... YOUR NAME ISN'T PRUDENCE, IS IT?

RAT-A-TAT TAT BOM BABOM

MARY WAS A DYKE

UH... IT USED TO BE. WHO ARE Y... OH MY GOD! **SISTER MARY MAGDALEN?**

IT'S FRANKIE NOW, DEAR. I LEFT THE ORDER YEARS AGO. ARE YOU STILL DRAWING NAKED LADIES IN YOUR CATECHISM?

Au Courant

©1994 BY ALISON BECHDEL

193

HEY, COOL BOOTS, LOIS.

YEAH. I GOT 'EM FROM AN AUSTRALIAN SHOT-PUTTER AT THE GAMES.

TEAM HELSINKI!

I SWAPPED HER MY DOC MARTENS. I WAS GLAD TO GET RID OF 'EM NOW THAT EVERY SUBURBAN MALL CRAWLER HAS A PAIR.

!

MADWIMMIN BOOKS

IGNITE THE RIOT

OH, JEEZ. HERE'S A SUBMISSION FOR "MADWIMMIN READ" FROM SOMEONE NAMED JILLIAN WHO IDENTIFIES AS A TRANSSEXUAL LESBIAN.

COOL.

GO HOMOS NY TEAM AQUATICS

THE COVER LETTER SAYS "I HOPE YOU'LL CONSIDER CHANGING THE NAME OF YOUR READING SERIES FOR LOCAL LESBIAN WRITERS TO BE INCLUSIVE OF TRANSGENDER AND BISEXUAL WOMEN WRITERS TOO." OH, MAN!

GUESS IT'S TIME TO GET WITH THE PROGRAM, HUH?

ACT UP BRUXELLES

WHAT AM I SUPPOSED TO DO? HAVE BI WOMEN AND DRAG QUEENS COME IN HERE AND READ ABOUT SCHTUPPING THEIR BOYFRIENDS?

WHY NOT? I'M SURE THEY'D HAVE A UNIQUE PERSPECTIVE ON THE TOPIC.

LOIS, I'M STILL TRYING TO ADJUST TO LESBIANS USING DILDOS! WHAT AM I SUPPOSED TO MAKE OF A MAN WHO BECAME A WOMAN WHO'S ATTRACTED TO WOMEN?!

LOVE IS A MANY-GENDERED THING, PAL. GET USED TO IT.

WELL FINE. LET PEOPLE DO WHAT THEY WANT. BUT I'M NOT GONNA ADD THIS UNWIELDY "BISEXUAL AND TRANSGENDER" BUSINESS TO THE NAME OF MY READING SERIES. I DON'T EVEN KNOW WHAT TRANSGENDER MEANS!

SÃO PAOLO VOLLEYBALL

A TIP O' THE NIB TO JANIS WALWORTH!

IT'S SORT OF AN EVOLVING CONCEPT. I MEAN, WE HAVEN'T HAD ANY LANGUAGE FOR PEOPLE YOU CAN'T NEATLY PEG AS EITHER BOY OR GIRL.

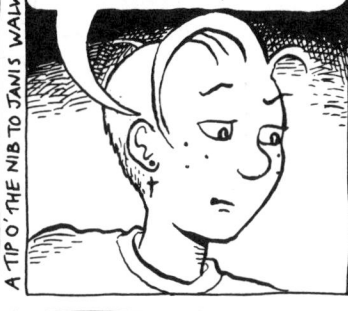

LIKE CROSS-DRESSERS, TRANSSEXUALS, PEOPLE WHO LIVE AS THE OPPOSITE SEX BUT DON'T HAVE SURGERY, DRAG QUEENS AND KINGS, AND ALL KINDS OF OTHER TRANSGRESSIVE FOLKS. "TRANSGENDER" IS A WAY TO UNITE EVERYONE INTO A GROUP, EVEN THOUGH ALL THESE PEOPLE MIGHT NOT SELF-IDENTIFY AS TRANSGENDER.

IN FACT, THE POINT IS THAT WE'RE ALL JUST OURSELVES, AND NOT CATEGORIES. INSTEAD OF TWO RIGID GENDERS, THERE'S AN INFINITE SEXUAL CONTINUUM! COOL, HUH?

HOW DO YOU KNOW ALL THIS STUFF?

GIRL JOCK

FROM HANGING OUT WITH JILLIAN AT LESBIAN AVENGERS MEETINGS. SHE TOLD ME SHE WAS GONNA SEND THIS TO YOU.

YOU LOVE TO WATCH ME SQUIRM, DON'T YOU?

LIME LIGHT

194

© 1994 BY ALISON BECHDEL

THANK YOU, JILLIAN, FOR THAT FASCINATING, UH, TRANSSEXUAL VERSION OF THE OEDIPUS LEGEND, "OEDIPAL COM**PLEX**." THANKS ALSO TO MIKO TAKAGI AND DEIRDRE TRIVELPIECE FOR SHARING THEIR WORK WITH US TONIGHT, AND TO OUR ASL INTERPRETER, JO PALMER.

AND THANKS TO ALL OF YOU FOR COMING OUT TO SUPPORT OUR LOCAL AUTHORS, AND MAKING THIS FIRST EVENT IN OUR "MADWIMMIN READ" SERIES A SUCCESS. PLEASE STICK AROUND FOR REFRESHMENTS, AND COME BACK AGAIN NEXT MONTH.

A TIP O' THE NIB TO LYNETTE REEP.

HUH! YOU PULLED IT OFF! NICE WORK, MO. AND LOOK AT ALL THESE PEOPLE! I BETTER GET UP TO THE REGISTER. YOU GO SCHMOOZE.

VERY IMPRESSIVE. NO ONE WOULD EVER SUSPECT YOU WERE A SHY PERSON, THE WAY YOU RAN THE SHOW.

EXCUSE ME. I JUST NEED TO SAY I WAS REALLY SHOCKED THAT YOU LET A **MAN** READ HERE TONIGHT. MEN HAVE ACCESS TO THE WHOLE WORLD. WHY SHOULD WE SHARE OUR MEAGER RESOURCES WITH THEM?

UH... WELL, FIRST OF ALL, HE'S NOT A MAN, HE'S A LESBIAN. I MEAN, **SHE'S** A LESBIAN. AND SECOND, I WANT THIS SERIES TO BE INCLUSIVE, AND NOT SOME PRIVATE CLUB. I MEAN, WHO AM I TO QUESTION SOMEONE ELSE'S IDENTITY?

NO PICNIC

© 1994 BY ALISON BECHDEL

(195)

Panel 1: IS IT AL- MOST DONE? I'VE GOTTA BE AT A MEETING IN AN HOUR.

JUST ABOUT. IS THIS FOR THE DOMESTIC PARTNERSHIP BENEFITS BILL?

Panel 2: YEAH. WE'VE GOT A PRETTY SOLID COALITION OF COMMUNITY GROUPS BEHIND US. NOW WE'RE GEARING UP FOR LOBBYING AND HEARINGS. YOU SHOULD THINK ABOUT TESTIFYING!

Panel 3: JEEZ, ELLEN. I CAN'T TAKE **ANYTHING** ELSE ON. I'M WORKING SIXTY HOUR WEEKS AS IT IS.

Panel 4: IT WOULD TAKE FIVE MINUTES! YOU COULD BRING RAFAEL UP TO THE PODIUM WITH YOU! IT'LL BE **PERFECT!**

Panel 5: COME ON! THE DOMESTIC PARTNERS REGISTRY IS A CRITICAL STEP TOWARDS GETTING OUR RELATION- SHIPS RECOGNIZED!

LOOK, I THINK IT'S GREAT YOU'RE DOING THIS, BUT GETTING THE GOVERNMENT INVOLVED IN MY PERSONAL LIFE IS NOT HIGH ON MY LIST OF PRIORITIES RIGHT NOW.

Panel 6: DID I TELL YOU I MIGHT BE GOING UP AGAINST THE UNION CARBUNCLE CHEM- ICAL CORPORATION? WE FOUND A L.U.S.T. AT THEIR SOUTH END PLANT, AND I THINK IT'S CONNECTED TO THE HIGH CANCER RATE OVER THERE.

A **LUST?**

Panel 7: LEAKY UNDER- GROUND STORAGE TANK. IT'S CON- TAMINATING THE GROUND WATER.

HEY, IF YOU'RE SO WORRIED ABOUT CONTAM- INATION, QUIT POKING MY TOFU WITH THAT CHICKEN FORK.

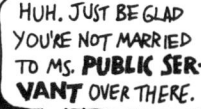

let them eat cake

©1994 BY ALISON BECHDEL (196)

Buzzed ON CAKE AND ICE CREAM, SEVERAL GUESTS AT RAFAEL'S FIRST BIRTHDAY PARTY HAVE REMAINED IN THE KITCHEN FOR SOME LIVELY DEBATE.

... WELL, WHAT GETS ME IS ALL THESE GAY **NEOCONS** CRAWLING OUT OF THE WOODWORK.

TELL ME ABOUT IT! A BUNCH OF WHITE GAY MEN TRYING TO CONVINCE THE HOMOPHOBES TO LIKE THEM BECAUSE THEY'RE JUST NORMAL, SEXIST, RACIST, GOD-FEARING, PROFIT-DRIVEN BOYS NEXT DOOR!

THE QUESTION IS, WOULD THESE LOG CABIN CLUB TYPES EVER HAVE COME OUT AT **ALL** IF **LEFTIST** QUEERS HADN'T BEEN FIGHTING FOR THEIR RIGHTS IN THE STREETS FOR THE PAST **25 YEARS?** I THINK **NOT.**

I DUNNO, MO. STREET ACTIVISTS AND DYKES ON BIKES ARE GREAT, BUT IT TAKES ALL KINDS! IF SOME STARCHED, STRAIGHT-ACTING GAY MEN AND LESBIANS WANT TO SUCK UP TO THE REPUBLICAN PARTY, IT CAN ONLY HELP!

YEAH... HELP **THEM.** THEY'LL SELL THE **REST** OF US DOWN THE RIVER JUST TO GET THEIR WINGTIPS IN THE DOOR! THEY'RE ANTI-CHOICE, ANTI-AFFIRMATIVE ACTION, PRO-BIG BUSINESS...

THEY PROBABLY **EAT VEAL!** THEY PROBABLY DON'T **RECYCLE!** THEY PROBABLY HAVE **WET DREAMS** ABOUT SKINNYDIPPING AT THE BOHEMIAN GROVE WITH **GEORGE WILL!**

OKAY, MO. I THINK YOU'VE HAD ENOUGH ICING.

Meanwhile, in the living room...

THANKS, LOIS. D'YOU THINK YOU COULD'VE FOUND A MORE IRRITATING GIFT?

WELL, IT WAS THIS OR THE TALKING STUFFED **BARNEY.**

BING DONG DINK DINK

XYLOPHONE

LET'S SEE WHAT YOUR FOLKS SENT, BABE! SMELLS LIKE MONEY.

RAFFI, NO! DON'T BONK STELLA! SORRY, GLORIA.

IT'S OKAY. SO TONI, DID YOU COME OUT TO YOUR PARENTS YET?

BAY-BEE!

NO... I WAS ALL READY TO, BUT THEN THE VATICAN MADE THEIR LITTLE PRONOUNCEMENT ABOUT HOW SAME SEX COUPLES SHOULDN'T BE ALLOWED TO ADOPT OR USE ALTERNATIVE INSEMINATION. MY MOM'S SO POPE-CRAZY, I THOUGHT I'D WAIT TILL THINGS QUIETED DOWN.

BONK.

HAVE A NICE WAIT.

A CHECK FOR RAFFI, A PHOTO OF THE NEIGHBORS' SON, JULIO, FOR YOU.

HUH. JULIO LOOKS A LITTLE LIGHT IN THE LOAFERS TO ME.

The kitchen crew is starting to crash...

SO WHAT MAKES SOME GAY PEOPLE TURN OUT TO BE REVOLUTIONARY ACTIVISTS, AND OTHERS TURN OUT TO BE SNIVELING COLLABORATIONISTS?

THE AMOUNT OF REFINED SUGAR THEIR MOTHERS ATE WHILE THEY WERE IN THE WOMB?

SOMEONE STOP ME. I CAN SEE BOB DOLE'S FACE IN THE BUTTER PECAN.

virtual interface

© 1994 BY ALISON BECHDEL

(197)

OUR HEROINE VENTURES INTO A LOCAL CAFFEINE DEN.

YOU'RE SURE THIS IS DECAF?

YEAH. ONE TWENTY-FIVE, PLEASE.

HEY GIRL! LOOKIN' GOOD!

'SUP, JULES? GIMME A DOUBLE MOCHA LATTE WITH A SHOT OF MANGO, SOME WHIPPED CREAM, AND A LITTLE CINNAMON.

CLINK!

TIPS

MO!

GRAB A CHAIR! WHAT'RE YOU DOING HERE?

HI! I JUST HAD MY "COMPUTERS FOR THE TECHNOLOGICALLY STUNTED" CLASS, AND I NEED TO UNWIND.

HOW'S THAT GOING?

AHH, I DUNNO. ALL THAT JARGON. I JUST CAN'T GRASP NEW STUFF LIKE I USED TO. I FEEL SO **OLD** LATELY.

JOIN THE CLUB. THE SEMESTER STARTED TODAY, AND I HAVE A WHOLE NEW RAFT OF FRESHMEN. I KEEP AGING AND THEY'RE ETERNALLY EIGHTEEN.

HAVE YOU NOTICED, SUDDENLY THERE'S ALL THESE **YOUNG DYKES** EVERYWHERE? WHERE'D THEY **COME** FROM?!

THE MALL?

61

BUFFED

© 1994 BY ALISON BECHDEL

ALL READY FOR YOUR BIG NIGHT, MO? D'YOU NEED ANY POINTERS? WANT ME TO COME OVER AND TAKE A **PICTURE** OF YOU TWO BEFORE YOU GO OUT?

OH, MY **GOD!** **YOU** HAVE A **DATE?**

NO, I DO **NOT** HAVE A DATE. UH... AND IF I **DID**, I WOULD RESENT THAT TONE OF VOICE.

198

ALL FREEDOM RINGS 80% OFF!

SHE'S GOING TO THE MOVIES WITH DEIRDRE, ONE OF THE WRITERS WHO READ HERE LAST MONTH.

REALLY! I LIKED HER. SHE WAS SMART. AND NOT UN-ATTRACTIVE, AS I RECALL.

SO MO, ARE YOU GONNA PUT OUT?

LOIS! THIS ISN'T A DATE! SHE JUST WANTS TO MEET MORE PEOPLE. AND IF IT **WAS** A DATE, I WOULD CERTAINLY **NOT** HAVE SEX WITH HER THE FIRST TIME WE WENT OUT!

CHLOE PLUS MIL-DRED

THE BOOK OF SHORT LESBIAN PENGUIN STORIES

WHOA! HAVE YOU SIGNED THE YOUTH FOR CHRIST "TRUE LOVE WAITS" CHASTITY PLEDGE?

NO, IT'S JUST... I'VE **DONE** THE U-HAUL SCENE, Y'KNOW? I'M TIRED OF GOING TO BED WITH A DATE AND WAKING UP WITH A DOMESTIC PARTNER. FROM NOW ON I'M GONNA WAIT UNTIL I KNOW THIS IS WHO I WANT TO BE WITH BEFORE I **SLEEP** WITH HER.

WHAT KIND OF TWISTED LOGIC IS THAT? HOW D'YOU KNOW YOU WANNA **BE** WITH HER UNLESS YOU **DO** HER?

LOIS, I'M NOT LIKE YOU. IF I HAVE SEX, I FALL IN LOVE. IT'S A GENETIC DEFECT.

MO, WHY ARE YOU SO SURE TONIGHT ISN'T A DATE?

OH, IT'S A DATE! THIS BABE DEIRDRE WAS **CREAMING** HER **JEANS** WHEN MO SAID SHE'D GO OUT WITH HER.

LOIS!

GO ON. GIVE HER A TUMBLE. SHE **WANTS** YOU.

LOOK. EVEN IF I WAS INTERESTED, I'D WANNA GO REALLY SLOW. I THINK IT WOULD BE EXCITING.

I WISH MAXINE AND I HAD DONE THAT. ONCE YOU GO ALL THE WAY, YOU CAN NEVER GET BACK THAT SUBLIME, TORTURED TENSION OF JUST HOLDING HANDS, OR THE FIRST TIME YOU UNBUTTON HER SHIRT.

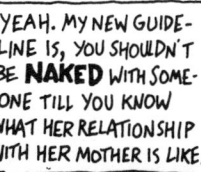

YEAH. MY NEW GUIDELINE IS, YOU SHOULDN'T BE **NAKED** WITH SOMEONE TILL YOU KNOW WHAT HER RELATIONSHIP WITH HER MOTHER IS LIKE.

GOOD POINT. IF I'D DONE THAT, I NEVER WOULD'VE TAKEN MY **COAT** OFF WITH MAXINE.

OKAY. I'M OUTTA HERE. I HAVE TO GO TO THE GYM BEFORE MY, UH... APPOINTMENT.

GO GIRL! WORK IT!

PUMP IT UP!

Shortly thereafter...

MO! I DIDN'T KNOW YOU WORKED OUT HERE! THIS IS MY MOM, BETTY. MOM, THIS IS WHO I'M GOING OUT WITH TONIGHT!

YMCA MOTHER-DAUGHTER SWIM MEET THIS SATURDAY!

NICE TO MEET YOU, MO. DEIRDRE'S SO LOOKING FORWARD TO YOUR DATE!

63

Mystery Date

199

*I*s it or isn't it? Despite strong circumstantial evidence, our heroine remains unconvinced that she is indeed on a date.

THALIA

LESBIAN/GAY/BI FILM FESTIVAL
OBSCURE NEW LESBIAN SHORTS 7
OPAQUE NEW GAY SHORTS 9
CAVALCADE O'BISEXUALS 11

SO, LIKE, ARE YOU SEEING ANYONE?

SEEING ANYONE? UH... NO. WELL, UNLESS YOU COUNT MY THERAPIST.

YOU'RE **SEEING** YOUR **THERAPIST**?

NO! I MEAN SEEING AS IN, "SEEING A THERAPIST," NOT LIKE I'M **SEEING** HER. IT'S A JOKE!

OH.

UM, SO... IT WAS REALLY NICE OF YOU TO GIVE ME YOUR EXTRA TICKET. I MEAN, CONSIDERING WE HARDLY KNOW EACH OTHER. I WISH I COULD BE MORE OUTGOING LIKE THAT. I GUESS I'D BE AFRAID PEOPLE WOULD THINK I WAS COMING ON TO THEM.

OH.

NOT THAT I THOUGHT THAT'S WHAT **YOU** WERE DOING. THAT'S WHAT I'M SAYING. IT WAS JUST REALLY **NICE**. UM, SO... THANKS.

LOOK, IS THIS OKAY?

EXIT

WHAT?

from the sublimation to the ridiculous

(200)

AFTER AN EVENING OF EXPERIMENTAL LESBIAN FILM, MO AND DEIRDRE'S QUASI-DATE CONTINUES OVER COFFEE.

I DIDN'T QUITE GET WHY THEY KEPT INTERCUTTING THE SEX SCENE WITH THAT FOOTAGE OF CHERNOBYL AFTER THE ACCIDENT, BUT IT WAS STILL PRETTY HOT.

UH... DOESN'T THAT STUFF KEEP YOU AWAKE?

THIS? I GUESS. BUT I'M NOT PLANNING ON GOING TO SLEEP ANYTIME SOON.

OH. UM... I GUESS YOU PROBABLY DO YOUR WRITING AT NIGHT, HUH?

NOT REALLY.

OH. HUH. SO... YOU'RE A MORNING PERSON, THEN?

THERE'S ONE WAY TO FIND OUT.

COFF! —SPLUTTER— UM... EXCUSE ME?

OKAY, MO. I GIVE UP. IS IT JUST THAT YOU'RE NOT INTERESTED, OR ARE YOU REALLY THIS DENSE?

IN-IN- INTERESTED? UH... LIKE... YOU MEAN, IN YOU? JEEZ, DEIRDRE. I DUNNO. I MEAN, I... I...

OH, SHIT. LOOK, FORGET IT. I'M SORRY. I THOUGHT YOU WERE JUST NEUROTICALLY SHY. I GUESS I'M THE DENSE ONE.

NO, YOU'RE NOT! IT'S **ME**. **I'M** DENSE! **DENSE** AND **NEUROTIC!**

UH... LET'S GO SOMEPLACE WHERE WE CAN TALK.

𝓔FTSOONS, AT MO'S BACHELOR DIGS...

...AND IT'S JUST BEEN SO LONG, I'VE FORGOTTEN HOW TO **ACT**, Y'KNOW? I FEEL SO CONFUSED! IT'S NOT THAT I DON'T FIND YOU ATTRACTIVE, IT'S JUST THAT...

I'M REALLY **WORRIED** ABOUT THE POSSIBILITY OF A **REPUBLICAN, RELIGIOUS RIGHT-BACKED WHITE HOUSE** IN 96!

I MEAN, WHILE CLINTON FLOUNDERS AND THE GAY RIGHTS MOVEMENT HAS NO DONORS AND NO LEADERS, THE **CHRISTIAN COALITION** GROWS BY **LEAPS** AND **BOUNDS!**

THE COUNTRY IS SLIPPING INTO A CONSER-VATIVE **COMA!** PEOPLE WOULD RATHER BASH IMMIGRANTS, BLAME QUEERS, AND BUILD BIGGER PRISONS THAN FACE THE **REAL** PROBLEMS: THE WIDENING GULF BETWEEN RICH AND POOR! UNTRAMMELED CORPORATE GREED! AND, UH... **WAL-MART!**

I THINK THOSE ARE LIKE, ALL THE SAME THING.

CALL ME WHEN YOU WORK IT ALL OUT, OKAY?

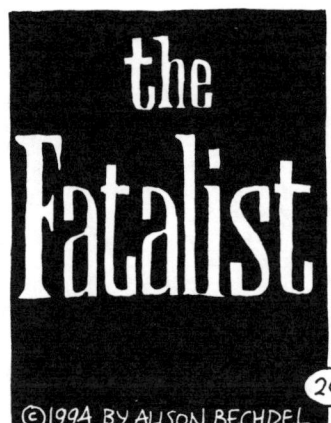

the Fatalist

©1994 BY ALISON BECHDEL

201

YEAH? AND **THEN** WHAT?

AND THEN SHE KISSED ME.

HAH! THEA OWES ME FIVE BUCKS!

WHOA! SHE JUST, LIKE, KISSED YOU? WHAT DID **YOU** DO?

I DUNNO! I MEAN, WHAT COULD I DO? I KISSED HER BACK. SHE TOOK ME BY SURPRISE.

WHAT KIND OF KISS ARE WE TALKING HERE? POLITE PECK? SISTERLY SMOOCH? OR A REAL SPITSWAPPER?

IT WAS...YOU KNOW, A REGULAR KISS. SHE TASTED LIKE POPCORN AND VIENNESE ROAST.

THEN WHAT HAPPENED?

THEN SHE LEFT.

LET ME GUESS. YOU DIDN'T TRY TO STOP HER.

SHE WAS READY TO GO.

MO, D'YOU MIND IF I INCLUDE THIS STORY IN THE PAPER I'M PRESENTING AT THE QUEER THEORY CONFERENCE NEXT WEEK?

RING!

CRUNCH

I'M LOOKING AT HOW THE HYPERSEXUALIZED PERSONAE OF BLACK WOMEN AND LESBIANS IN THE MALE LITERARY CANON CONTRAST WITH OUR ACTUAL EXPERIENCES OF DESIRE, FOCUSING ON INTERSUBJECTIVE MODALITIES OF **LESBIAN IMPOTENCE.**

YOU KNOW WHAT'S WRONG WITH YOU, MO? YOU'RE AFRAID OF LETTING ANYTHING **GOOD** HAPPEN.

RING

OF COURSE I AM! AS SOON AS SOMETHING GOOD HAPPENS, SOMETHING **BAD** IS RIGHT AROUND THE CORNER!

ARE YOU STILL IN THERAPY? AND WHAT ABOUT THIS DEIRDRE? IS SHE PRE-SHRUNK?

JEEZIZ, SPARROW! IT WAS OUR FIRST DATE! I DIDN'T TAKE HER MENTAL HEALTH HISTORY!

WELL DON'T COME CRYING TO ME WHEN YOU FIND OUT SHE STILL THINKS SHE HAD A HAPPY CHILDHOOD.

MO, THAT WAS JEZANNA ON THE PHONE. SHE WANTS US TO COME OVER TO THE BOOKSTORE TONIGHT. RIGHT NOW, IF WE CAN.

WHAT'S WRONG?!

HER MOM IS REALLY SICK, SO SHE HAS TO FLY HOME. SHE WANTS TO GO OVER STUFF AT WORK WITH US BEFORE HER FLIGHT LEAVES.

WHAT'S THE MATTER WITH HER MOTHER? DID SHE SAY?

NO. SHE SOUNDED PRETTY UPSET, THOUGH.

MAYBE I SHOULD COME WITH YOU, IN CASE SHE NEEDS TO TALK. I MEAN, MY MOM'S BEEN SICK A LOT. DO YOU THINK SHE'D MIND?

PROBABLY. BUT IT'S WORTH A TRY. LET'S GO.

the rock

©1994 BY ALISON BECHDEL

202

... SO ARE YOU TWO CLEAR ON WHAT YOUR JOBS ARE WHILE I'M GONE?

YEAH.

GOT IT.

I'M GONNA HAVE TONI COME IN AND DO THE BOOKKEEPING AND PAY-ROLL, BUT MO IS RESPONSIBLE FOR EVERYTHING ELSE: MEETING WITH SALES REPS, ORDERING, PAYING BILLS, MAKING DEPOSITS, DOING THE SCHEDULE, ALL THAT. I WANT THE THREE OF YOU TO WORK TOGETHER, BUT IF YOU CAN'T, MO'S THE BOSS. OKAY?

MIMMIWAAM

MMIWAAM BOOKS

GULP!

JEZANNA, YOU SOUND LIKE YOU'RE NEVER COMING BACK! THIS IS JUST FOR A LITTLE WHILE, RIGHT?

OH! AND WE'RE OUT OF TOILET PAPER, AND THE SPIRITUALITY SECTION NEEDS RE-ALPHABET-IZING. Y'KNOW, MAYBE I SHOULD WRITE UP A DETAILED LIST OF ALL THE THINGS YOU'LL HAVE TO...

JEZ, WE'LL FIGURE IT OUT! DESPITE THE FACT THAT YOU'RE A TOTAL CON-TROL FREAK, AND DO ALL THE IMPOR-TANT STUFF AROUND HERE YOURSELF, I THINK WE'VE MANAGED TO PICK UP A THING OR TWO BY OSMOSIS.

DON'T WORRY ABOUT THE STORE! YOU NEED TO TAKE CARE OF **YOUR-SELF** IF YOU'RE GONNA BE ANY USE TO YOUR MOTH-ER. NOW, ARE YOU OKAY?

JEZANNA! I CAME RIGHT OVER! ARE YOU OKAY? WHAT HAPPENED?

70

HI, TONI. I JUST FOUND OUT MY MOTHER HAS BREAST CANCER, AND I'M FLYING OUT TO BE WITH HER TOMORROW. COME ON, LET'S GO OVER THE BOOKS. I HAVE A LOT TO DO TONIGHT.

BREAST CANCER?! HOLD ON, JEZ! LET'S TALK ABOUT THIS! ARE YOU OKAY?

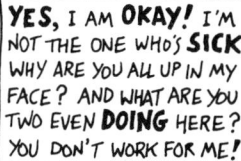

YES, I AM OKAY! I'M NOT THE ONE WHO'S SICK. WHY ARE YOU ALL UP IN MY FACE? AND WHAT ARE YOU TWO EVEN DOING HERE? YOU DON'T WORK FOR ME!

WE'RE YOUR FRIENDS. THIS IS WHAT FRIENDS DO.

LISTEN. MY MOM'S HAD CANCER FOR FIVE YEARS NOW. I CAN HELP YOU DEAL WITH THIS IF YOU WANT TO TALK.

THERE'S NOTHING LEFT TO SAY! I TOLD HER A THOUSAND TIMES, "MAMA! YOU NEED TO GET A MAMMOGRAM!" I EVEN MADE APPOINTMENTS! DID SHE KEEP THEM? NO, SHE DID NOT!

ONE DAY SHE NOTICED A LUMP! DID SHE TELL ANYONE? NO, SHE DID NOT! DIDN'T WANT TO BE ANY TROUBLE! THEY ONLY FOUND IT SIX MONTHS LATER WHEN MY COUSIN DRAGGED HER IN FOR A PHYSICAL!

YOU'RE ANGRY. THAT'S GOOD. STAY WITH YOUR FEELINGS.

HEY! IF YOU THINK I'M GONNA BREAK DOWN BAWLING SO YOU CAN ALL MAKE A FUSS, YOU GOT ANOTHER THINK COMING. LET'S GO, TONI!

HOW BAD IS IT?

THEY DON'T KNOW YET. OR SHE JUST WON'T SAY.

UNDERNEATH THE ATTITUDE, SHE'S REALLY SCARED.

YEAH, SHE IS IN SO MUCH DENIAL. COME ON, LET'S GET THESE BOOKS RE-ALPHABETIZED!

THE BLACK WOMEN'S HEALTH BOOK

MY MOTHER / SELF

minding the store

© 1994 BY ALISON BECHDEL

RIGHT.... OKAY.... WELL LISTEN, I'M REALLY GLAD YOUR MOM MADE IT THROUGH THE SURGERY ALL RIGHT. HANG IN THERE, JEZ, AND I'LL TALK TO YOU TOMORROW.... **YES**, THE STORE IS **FINE**. I'VE GOT EVERYTHING UNDER CONTROL. DON'T WORRY! OKAY, BYE.

203

EXCUSE ME. I'M LOOKING FOR A COPY OF THAT NEW BOOK, "STRANGE JUSTICE: THE SELLING OF CLARENCE THOMAS."

SURE! WE JUST GOT A SHIPMENT IN THIS MORNING. LEMME GET YOU ONE.

HEY, MO. CHECK IT OUT. THEY SENT US THE **WRONG** NEW CLARENCE THOMAS BOOK. WE HAVE THIRTY COPIES HERE OF THE WACKO ONE BY SENATOR DANFORTH!

HOW'D **THAT** HAPPEN? SHIT! I'VE GOT A CUSTOMER OUT THERE WAITING FOR THE RIGHT ONE!

RESURRECTION JOHN DANFORTH

ISN'T THERE A DISPLAY COPY IN THE WINDOW? SELL THAT.

GOOD THINKING!

RESURRECTION

AAUGH!

HEATHER'S MOMMIES WEAR ARMY BOOTS

CAMILLE PAGLIA

SIMPS 'N PIMPS

(TIP O' THE NIB TO KATHLEEN DE BOLD)

Trouble

©1994 BY ALISON BECHDEL

204

HEY, LOIS. ARE YOU CLOSING? I THOUGHT YOU GUYS WERE OPEN TILL EIGHT TONIGHT.

NO, SORRY. BUT GO ON IN, MO'S STILL HERE. I GOTTA RUN. THE AVENGERS ARE PLANNING AN ACTION AGAINST THE REPUBLICANS' **CONTRACT "ON" AMERICA.**

MADWIMMIN BOOKS

JILLIAN'S GONNA PUT ON A NEWT GINGRICH MASK, DRIVE BY IN A LIMO, AND MOW US ALL DOWN WITH A TOY UZI. WE HAVE FAKE BLOOD AND EVERYTHING.

HI, MO. I WAS IN THE NEIGHBORHOOD. I THOUGHT I'D SEE IF YOU WANTED TO GO GET SOMETHING TO EAT.

UH... HI, DEIRDRE. JEEZ, I CAN'T. I HAFTA WRITE A BOOK REVIEW FOR THE TRIBUNE TONIGHT, AND I HAVEN'T EVEN STARTED IT YET.

WHAT BOOK? WE CAN TALK ABOUT IT OVER DINNER. YOU GOTTA EAT, RIGHT?

ZIP

CO-OP CREDIT UNION

NO, I REALLY HAVE TO GO HOME AND GET TO WORK. IT'S A NEW LESBIAN EROTICA COLLECTION. I'M GONNA DISCUSS IT IN THE CONTEXT OF OUR EROTOPHOBIC SOCIETY AND CLINTON'S FIRING OF JOYCELYN ELDERS FOR MENTIONING **MASTURBATION.**

THAT GUY IS SO GUTLESS! I MEAN, WHAT'S HE TRYING TO PROVE BY CANNING THE ONLY PERSON IN WASHINGTON WITH ANY INTEGRITY? DOES HE THINK THAT'S GONNA WIN BACK ALL THE ANGRY WHITE MEN WHO VOTED REPUBLICAN THIS FALL?

OUT   OFFICE

74

HE'D DO A LOT BETTER BY TAKING A **STAND** FOR ONCE. IF PEOPLE WANT A CONSERVATIVE PRESIDENT IN '96, THEY'LL VOTE FOR A **REAL** ONE.

CLINTON'S ALREADY LOST VOTES OVER THE MILITARY FIASCO. **ONE** IN **THREE** GAY VOTERS PICKED REPUBLICANS IN THE LAST ELECTION!

THE **FOOLS!** YOU CAN BET YOUR BUMPERSTICKERS THEY'RE MOSTLY WHITE GAY MEN WITH BUCKS, HAPPY TO SELL OUT IMMIGRANTS AND SINGLE MOTHERS ON WELFARE FOR A CHANCE AT A FUCKING **TAX BREAK.**

WHEN ARE PEOPLE GONNA LEARN? WE'VE GOTTA STICK TOGETHER IF WE EVER HOPE TO HAVE ANY REAL POWER IN THIS COUNTRY!

OFFICE

SO LIKE, WHAT'D YOU THINK OF THE BOOK?

I, UM... HAVEN'T READ IT YET.

MAYBE I CAN HELP YOU WITH YOUR RESEARCH. THOSE BOOKS ALWAYS INCLUDE A STORY ABOUT WOMEN HAVING SEX AT THE OFFICE.

UH... YES, I THINK YOU'RE RIGHT.

GASP.

OOF.

MOAN.

CRASH!

Flagrante Delicto

©1994 BY ALISON BECHDEL

... THEN AFTER AN UPDATE FROM THE FUNDRAISING COMMITTEE, LOIS IS GONNA READ THE DRAFT OF THE FACT SHEET WE'LL BE PASSING OUT AT THE ACTION.

OH, NO. I LEFT IT AT WORK!

WE **HAFTA** FINALIZE THAT THING TONIGHT. TOMORROW'S MY LAST DAY TEMPING AT THE LAW FIRM AND I DON'T KNOW WHERE ELSE I CAN SCAM FREE COPIES.

205

MEANWHILE, AT THE BOOKSTORE...

UH... DEIRDRE.. I SHOULD REALLY BE GETTING TO WORK ON THAT, UM... BOOK REVIEW.

CLIK

FORGET ABOUT THE BOOK REVIEW.

OFFICE

?

MYSTERIES

the nightly grind

©1995 BY ALISON BECHDEL

206

RAFAEL! MAMA HASN'T SEEN YOU IN TWO DAYS!

I WAS JUST PUTTING HIM TO BED. I THOUGHT HE'D NAP AT MADWIMMIN WHILE I DID THE PAYROLL, BUT LOIS GOT HIM TOO WORKED UP. THEN LATER, GLORIA BROUGHT STELLA OVER TO PLAY.

HE CAN'T GO TO BED! IT'S ONLY SEVEN! I LEFT A TON OF WORK UNFINISHED JUST SO I'D GET TO SPEND SOME TIME WITH HIM!

WHINE.

TOO BAD. YOU'LL JUST HAVE TO WASTE YOUR EVENING SPENDING TIME WITH ME.

LOOK, I'M SORRY. YOU KNOW I'M UNDER A LOT OF PRESSURE WITH THE UNION CARBUNCLE SUIT. HAS HE NURSED?

DON'T SAY THAT WORD! I TOLD YOU, HE'S FINALLY WEANED OFF THE BEDTIME FEEDING. I'M FREE! HAVEN'T YOU NOTICED, MY BREASTS ARE RETURNING TO THEIR NORMAL SIZE?

JEEZ, HE'S TOTALLY PASSED OUT.

GIVE HIM THAT TARANTULA. HE'LL CRY WITHOUT IT.

G'NIGHT, MONKEY BOY.

SLEEP TIGHT. TILL AROUND NOON, OKAY?

78

CLARICE, I'M THINKING ABOUT WORKING MORE. IT'S BEEN SO NICE GETTING OUT OF THE HOUSE TO DO THE BOOKS AT MADWIMMIN.

CLIK!

DID I TELL YOU WHAT A MESS JEZANNA'S BOOKKEEPING WAS? I GUESS IT WORKED FOR HER, BUT I'VE OVERHAULED THE WHOLE SYSTEM WHILE SHE'S BEEN GONE. SHE'LL BE SO PLEASED.

UH-HUH. WHAT'S THE LATEST ON HER MOTHER?

NOT GREAT. IT TURNS OUT SHE HAD TWO DIFFERENT TUMORS. AND THE CANCER WAS, LIKE, IN HER LYMPH NODES OR SOMETHING. SHE'LL PROBABLY HAVE TO DO CHEMO.

JESUS! IT MAKES ME SO ANGRY! I'VE SPENT ALL WEEK REVIEWING MEDICAL HISTORIES OF PEOPLE IN THE SOUTH END. THEY'VE GOT THE HIGHEST CANCER RATE IN THE CITY, AND...

FWIP!

ODDLY ENOUGH, THEY'VE ALSO GOT THE MOST CHEMICAL PLANTS AND WASTE DUMPS! MEANWHILE, INSTEAD OF LOOKING FOR WAYS TO PREVENT CANCER, LIKE... OH, I DUNNO! CEASING TO PUMP THE ENVIRONMENT FULL OF CARCINOGENS, MAYBE, WE SPEND ZILLIONS ON CANCER "MANAGEMENT!"

RING!

WHY? BECAUSE ALL THE CHEMICAL AND DRUG AND OIL COMPANY EXECS ON THE BOARDS OF ALL THE CANCER ORGANIZATIONS DON'T SEE AN ENVIRONMENTAL LINK!

HELLO?... HI, MO. WHAT'S UP?... WHAT?...MADWIMMIN'S RENT CHECK BOUNCED? BUT THERE WAS PLENTY IN THE ACCOUNT! ...OKAY. YEAH. I'LL COME BY FIRST THING AND FIGURE OUT WHAT WENT WRONG. SORRY!

COMPLETELY OVERHAULED THE SYSTEM, HUH?

SHUT UP.

unconsummate professionals

© 1995 BY ALISON BECHDEL

(207)

I CAN'T BELIEVE THE RENT CHECK BOUNCED! JEZANNA'S GONNA **FLIP!** WHILE SHE'S OFF TENDING HER SICK MOTHER, WE'RE RUNNING HER STORE INTO THE GROUND!

CALM **DOWN**, MO. I'LL FIGURE IT OUT. WHERE'S THE RECEIPT FOR THE DEPOSIT YOU MADE ON THE THIRTIETH?

UM... IT'S NOT THERE? JEEZ.

OFFICE

HEY, MO. THEY JUST DELIVERED THE **TRIBUNE** WITH YOUR REVIEW IN IT! CHECK IT OUT. "SAPPHIC STROKE BOOK SATISFIES."

10% Tribune
DICK ARMEY TO BARNEY FRANK: "I'M SORRY I CALLED YOU BARNEY FAG."

OH MY GOD!

YEAH. LOOKS LIKE THEY EDITED OUT A LOT OF YOUR CONTEXTUALIZING POLITICAL ANALYSIS.

10% Tribune
FRANK TO ARMEY: "NO PROBLEM, DICK. I MEAN, DICK."

NO, I MEAN THE DEPOSIT! I NEVER MADE IT!

A TIP O' THE NIB TO AMY RUBIN

IT'S, UH... BEEN LYING ON THE FLOOR ALL THIS TIME.

WHAT? MO, I WAS AWAKE ALL NIGHT WONDERING HOW I'D SCREWED THE BOOKS UP! HOW COULD YOU DO SOMETHING SO **STUPID?**

I BET YOU KICKED IT UNDER THERE LAST WEEK WHEN YOU AND DEIRDRE WERE ROLLING AROUND HALF-NAKED, HUH, MO?

CO-OP CREDIT UNION

80

HALF-NAKED?! WHO'S DEIRDRE?

UH... I HAFTA GET THIS TO THE CREDIT UNION **NOW**. CAN YOU DRIVE ME, LOIS?

MO, WAIT! DID YOU ORDER A HUNDRED COPIES OF THIS SIXTY-DOLLAR "BOB AND ROD" COFFEE TABLE BOOK?

OH, SHIT! I'LL DEAL WITH IT WHEN I GET BACK.

OKAY, GLORIA. I'M ALL DONE. LET'S PUT THEIR SNOWSUITS BACK ON AND GO TO THE PARK.

MUM-MUM.

SO WHO'S MO BEEN ROLLING AROUND NAKED WITH? SOUNDS PRETTY HOT.

YEAH, I'LL HAVE TO CALL LOIS LATER FOR THE DE- TAILS. JEEZ, I CAN'T REMEMBER THE LAST TIME I HAD SEX IN A SEMI-PUBLIC PLACE.

TELL ME ABOUT IT. I KNEW HAVING A KID WOULD CHANGE THINGS, BUT I NEVER EX- PECTED ANA AND I WOULD BECOME A LESBIAN BED DEATH STATISTIC.

LOIS, I CAN'T SEEM TO DO THE **SIMPLEST** THINGS RIGHT LATELY! WHAT IS **WRONG** WITH ME?

NOTHING GETTING FUCKED SILLY WON'T FIX. EVERY- ONE KNOWS, BRAIN CELLS DIE OFF MUCH MORE QUICKLY IN THE ABSENCE OF REGULAR, STRENUOUS SEXUAL ACTIVITY.

REALLY?

MO, DO US ALL A FAVOR AND ASK DEIRDRE OVER FOR SUCCOTASH OR SOMETHING. **SOON.**

the media event

© 1995 BY ALISON BECHDEL

208

A BLEAK WINTER'S EVE FINDS OUR VARIOUS HEROINES ENGAGED IN AN EVEN **BLEAKER** COMMON PURSUIT.

*J*EZANNA'S MOTHER IS STILL IN THE HOSPITAL.

WE NOW REJOIN THE SIMPSON TRIAL...

YOU CAN'T TRUST THOSE L.A. POLICE! THE MAN WAS FRAMED. HE'S INNOCENT!

I WANT TO TELL YOU O.J. SIMPSON

Z.

DAD. EVEN IF HE **DIDN'T** MURDER HER, I'D HARDLY CALL A WIFE-BEATER "INNOCENT." AND I CAN'T BELIEVE YOU BOUGHT HIS DAMN BOOK!

AIN'T I A WOMAN? bell hooks

WHO CHANGED THE CHANNEL? PUT "REAL STORIES OF THE HIGHWAY PATROL" BACK ON!

I JUST POINTED OUT THE BLOOD SO HE WOULDN'T STEP IN IT.

IT'S OVER, MAMA. DON'T WORRY. THIS IS MORBID AND VOYEURISTIC TOO.

*T*ONI AND GLORIA HAVE A LOT IN COMMON.

I THOUGHT YOU TWO HAD THIS GREAT SEX LIFE!

WE **USED** TO. I LOST INTEREST FOR A WHILE AFTER RAFFI WAS BORN, BUT LATELY I REALLY WANT IT AND CLARICE IS EITHER BUSY OR TIRED.

OFFICER, WHEN YOU FIRST SAW THE ICE CREAM, IT WASN'T MELTED?

ANA AND ME ARE LUCKY IF WE DO IT QUARTERLY.

HOW DOES SOMETHING SO **FUN** BECOME SUCH A PROBLEM? GOD, I MISS IT.

IT WAS MELTING. IT WAS HALF MELTED.

post coitum tristis[1]

[1] a certain melancholy sometimes experienced after sex.

© 1995 BY ALISON BECHDEL

209

UH...D'YOU HAVE A ROBE OR SOMETHING I CAN WEAR TO THE BATHROOM?

TAKE THE SHIRT ON THE DOOR.

SLAM!

OH, **GOD.** WHAT HAVE I **DONE?**

I WAS GONNA **HOLD HANDS!** TAKE IT **SLOW!** WAIT TILL I KNEW THIS WAS **IT!**

BUT **NO!** I GO ALL THE WAY ON THE THIRD... OR WAS IT THE SECOND DATE?

I SWORE I'D NEVER DO THIS AGAIN! SEX IS LIKE **GLUE.** NOW I'M **STUCK** TO DEIRDRE. **BONDED.**

FLUSH!

WE'LL PROBABLY BE SHOPPING FOR A HOUSE IN THE SUBURBS BEFORE THE WEEK IS OUT, AND FOR ALL I KNOW SHE'S A **MEAT EATER,** OR A COUNTRY-WESTERN **DANCE FIEND,** OR **WORSE.**

HMM... SHE SMELLS LIKE TOMATO - APRICOT CHUTNEY.

BUT IF **I'M** INCAPABLE OF OVERCOMING MY ANIMAL INSTINCTS DESPITE MY BETTER JUDGMENT, WHAT HOPE IS THERE FOR **HUMANITY AT LARGE?**

CONSERVATIVE POLITICIANS THRIVE BY PANDERING TO PEOPLE'S BASEST FEARS! HOMOPHOBIC AND ANTI-IMMIGRANT REFERENDA GET PASSED BY POPULAR VOTE!

SOUTHERN STATES WANT TO BRING BACK **FLOGGING** TO "CONTROL THE CRIME RATE," AND GOD-FEARING, DIFFERENCE-HATING **GUN NUTS** ARE FORMING **CITIZEN MILITIAS** ALL OVER THE COUNTRY!

A LITTLE RUSH HERE, A LITTLE NEWT THERE, AND PEOPLE STAMPEDE LIKE ANIMALS, TRAMPLING CIVIL RIGHTS AND HUMANIST DISCOURSE IN A PANIC-DRIVEN **FRENZY** OF **MOB RULE!**

KNOCK KNOCK!

YOU HAVE TO JIGGLE THE HANDLE AFTER YOU FLUSH. LOOK, WE FORGOT ABOUT OUR ICE CREAM. IT'S ALL MELTED.

ON THE OTHER HAND, IF SHE WANTS TO DO AN OCCASIONAL LINE DANCE OR EAT THE ODD PORK CHOP, MAYBE I COULD ADJUST.

DRAGNET

©1995 BY ALISON BECHDEL

*L*OIS HAS PROMISED TO DO A BACKGROUND CHECK ON DEIRDRE FOR MO.

2/1

CURLY-HAIRED CHICK? YEAH... I DID HER ONCE A YEAR OR SO AGO. I GUESS I WENT A TAD SHORTER THAN SHE LIKED. DIDN'T SHE READ HER STUFF AT THE BOOKSTORE THE SAME NIGHT I DID?

BZZZZZZZ

I DON'T THINK SHE QUITE PULLS OFF THAT FIRST PERSON, PRESENT TENSE PROSE STYLE. SHE'S IN THE SAME WRITER'S GROUP AS JULES, THE JAVA JERK AT THE CAFÉ ACROSS THE STREET.

ZZZZZ

WHO WANTS TO KNOW?

RELAX. A FRIEND OF MINE IS DATING HER. I JUST WANNA MAKE SURE SHE'S NOT AN AXE MURDER-ESS.

SCHZZK!

NO, SHE'S COOL. THAT'S GOOD SHE'S DATING. HER LAST GIRLFRIEND REALLY PUT HER THROUGH THE MILL.

OH **REALLY?**

BABE, DO YOU KNOW A WOMAN NAMED LOUISE, SLINGS HASH AT THE RIGHTEOUS TURNIP?

YEAH. BIG, STRAPPING GIRL, REALLY CUTE. SHE'S ALWAYS COMING IN TO SEE ANGELA WITH SOME KIND OF SPORTS INJURY. I THINK SHE PLAYS SOCCER.

SURE, I KNOW LOUISE. SHE'S OUR GOALIE.

WHAT DO YOU KNOW ABOUT HER EX, DEIRDRE? WHEN DID THEY BREAK UP?

THEY BROKE UP? AW, THAT'S TOO BAD! JEEZ, THEY WERE TOGETHER LIKE FIVE YEARS OR SOMETHING. WHICH ONE ARE YOU AFTER?

NEITHER, I'M JUST DOING A LITTLE PRO BONO WORK.

LESBIAN AVENGERS

DEMAND LESBIAN HEALTH RESEARCH MARCH & RALLY

SO HOW CAN I GET THE DETAILS?

I'M GOING TO A PARTY AFTER THIS WHERE PEOPLE MIGHT KNOW. WHY DON'T YOU COME ALONG?

LOIS! NO INFORMATION YET, BUT IF YOU WANNA CHECK LOUISE OUT, SHE'S HERE. LOOK FOR A TALL JOCK TYPE WITH A BANDANA ON HER HEAD.

TEAM DRESCH

SHE'S AMAZING HER WORDS SAVE ME

SOUTH LONDON STUDS

SHE HOLDS HER HEAD AS IF IT'S TRUTH

*L*ATER THAT MORNING...

ANOMIC CAFÉ

©1995 BY ALISON BECHDEL

(2/3)

*Our heroine has been swigging a pungent blend of mocha java and **WELTSCHMERZ**, topped with a dusting of **ANOMIE**.*

GIMME ANOTHER SHOT.

UH... HOW 'BOUT SOME DECAF THIS TIME?

DID I **ASK** FOR DECAF?

OKAY, OKAY. IT'S YOUR CENTRAL NERVOUS SYSTEM.

#8

JAVA JONES

REPUBLICANS PROPOSE PRIVATIZING CONGRESS

MO! THE BOOKSTORE'S JAMMED, AND THE REP FROM FURRIER, SPROUT & GENOUX IS WAITING TO SEE YOU! YOUR COFFEE BREAK WAS OVER 40 MINUTES AGO!

I CAN'T FACE IT ANY MORE, LOIS!

NO MORE FREE RIDE FOR POOR SINGLE MOMS

FACE WHAT?

ALL DURING THE REAGAN YEARS, I CONSOLED MYSELF WITH THE THOUGHT THAT IT WAS CONSERVATISM'S **LAST GASP**...THAT SLOWLY BUT SURELY WE WERE PROGRESSING TOWARD A MORE COMPASSIONATE, EGALITARIAN SOCIETY. BUT I WAS **NAIVE**.

$500 PER CHILD TAX CREDIT FOR RICH FAMILIES

92

NAIVE, DO YOU **HEAR** ME?!

I CAN SEE CLEARLY NOW. I'VE NEVER BEEN SO **LUCID**. DID YOU KNOW THE O.J. SIMPSON TRIAL IS REALLY AN ELABORATE REPUBLICAN **RUSE** TO DIVERT OUR ATTENTION WHILE THEY LEGISLATE US BACK TO THE **FEUDAL SYSTEM**?!

THEN WHILE WE'RE DISTRACTED TRYING TO **SURVIVE**, THE LUNATIC FRINGE BECOMES THE LUNATIC **MAINSTREAM!** NAZI SKINHEADS, CHRISTIAN FUNDAMENTALISTS AND GUN FREAKS WILL DRAG US ALL WITH THEM INTO A **BRAVE NEW SEVENTH CIRCLE OF HELL!**

MAYBE SO. BUT I'M GONNA GO GET YOU A POT OF SLEEPYTIME.

SLEEPYTIME?! WHO CAN SLEEP IN A WORLD FULL OF **TEC-9-TOTING TALK RADIO LISTENERS** WHO'D **BLOW YOUR HEAD** OFF AS SOON AS **SPIT** AT YOU?

MOB RULE CHEAPER THAN GOV'T

I'M GOING ON AN **ESPRESSO FAST**. IF TRUTH EXISTS, IT'S AT THE BOTTOM OF THIS DEMI-TASSE!

WELL, OKAY. BUT JEZANNA JUST CALLED FROM THE AIRPORT. SHE'S BACK FROM HER MOM'S AND SHE'S ON HER WAY TO THE STORE.

JEZANNA?

YOUR **BOSS**? THE ONE WHO LEFT YOU IN **CHARGE** WHILE SHE WAS AWAY? I BET THIS GOURMET COFFEE IS PRETTY PRICEY FOR SOMEONE ON UNEMPLOYMENT.

A DOUBLE ESPRESSO TO GO. UM... DECAF.

AND A CUP OF SLEEPYTIME.

93

The TANGO of ANGER

© 1995 BY ALISON BECHDEL

(214)

The BOSS IS BACK.

I SEE YOU DECIDED TO EXPAND OUR SELECTION OF GAY MEN'S EROTICA WHILE I WAS GONE, MO.

WHAT?! WE DON'T HAVE A MEN'S EROTICA SECTION!

BOOKS
PAGETURNERS
POTBOILERS

THEN WHY AM I LOOKING AT A BOX FULL OF VERY EXPENSIVE GYM QUEENS?

OH! I MADE A MISTAKE ON AN ORDER... I KEEP MEANING TO SEND THOSE BACK, BUT WE DON'T HAVE ANY PACKING TAPE.

BOB 'N ROD
$60

GIVE ME STRENGTH.

I'LL GET RIGHT ON IT, AS SOON AS I UNPACK THIS STUFF.

BOB 'N ROD

AND WHAT ARE ALL THESE RUGRATS DOING HERE? ARE WE OFFERING DAYCARE NOW?

NO, TONI AND HER FRIEND GLORIA BRING THEIR KIDS OVER WHILE TONI DOES THE PAYROLL. STELLA JUST STARTED WALKING.

SORRY, JEZ. THEY'RE A LITTLE WOUND UP. ARE YOU READY TO GO OVER THE BOOKS?

OKAY, LET'S SEE HOW YOU MANAGED.

TONI, WHAT **IS** ALL THIS? YOU CHANGED MY SYSTEM!

WELL, YEAH... I HAD A HARD TIME FOLLOWING IT, SO I SET UP A MORE, UH... CONVENTIONAL ONE. THIS WAY IT'LL BE EASIER TO PUT IT ON THE COMPUTER.

EXCUSE ME? DID I **ASK** YOU TO COMPUTERIZE MY BUSINESS? I **LIKED** THE OLD SYSTEM!

Y'KNOW, JEZANNA, MAYBE YOU SHOULD TAKE A FEW DAYS TO UNWIND BEFORE YOU JUMP BACK INTO THINGS HERE.

I'M **NEVER** LEAVING THIS STORE AGAIN! GOD KNOWS WHAT I'D COME BACK TO! DILDOES IN THE WINDOW DISPLAY, PROBABLY, AND ALTERNATIVE INSEMINATION CLINICS IN THE BACK ROOM!

LISTEN, I KNOW YOU'RE UPSET ABOUT YOUR MOTHER. DO YOU WANT TO TALK ABOUT IT? HOW'S SHE DOING?

MY MOTHER IS AN **UNREPENTANT** OLD **HARRIDAN.** AT HER WEAKEST WITH THE CHEMO, SHE MANAGED TO REMIND ME THAT IF I LOST WEIGHT, I MIGHT STILL BE ABLE TO FIND A HUSBAND.

SOUNDS LIKE SHE'S PROBABLY SCARED, AND JUST LASHING OUT AT WHOEVER'S HANDY.

TONI, IS RAFFI WITH YOU? I LOST SIGHT OF HIM!

RAFAEL!

RIP!

DAMMIT, MO! I HOPE YOU LIKE **BEEFCAKE**, GIRL, BECAUSE YOU JUST BOUGHT YOURSELF A COFFEE TABLE BOOK.

INTENTIONAL FAMILY VALUES

©1995 BY ALISON BECHDEL

(215)

YES!

TAP!

CLIK

SHH! I CAN'T BELIEVE WE FINALLY GOT THEIR NAPTIMES SYNCHRONIZED!

DON'T WORRY. IT WON'T LAST. WHAT'S FOR LUNCH?

UH... TEETHING BISCUITS AND A JUICE BOX?

SO GLORIA, I'M GONNA DO IT. I'M GONNA TELL MY PARENTS I'M A BIG DYKE.

WHAT ELSE IS NEW? YOU'VE BEEN GONNA TELL THEM EVER SINCE I MET YOU.

PEANUT BURR

NOW I REALLY MEAN IT. JEZANNA'S MOM HAVING CANCER GOT ME THINKING, Y'KNOW? WHO KNOWS HOW MUCH TIME WE HAVE LEFT?!

WELL, GREAT! I KNOW IT'S SCARY, BUT YOU CAN DO IT. BESIDES, WHAT'S THE WORST THAT COULD HAPPEN?

ARE YOU KIDDING? THEY COULD GO TO COURT LIKE SHARON BOTTOMS' MOM AND SUE FOR CUSTODY OF RAFFI, FOR STARTERS!

GOD, CAN YOU BELIEVE THAT CASE? THE VIRGINIA SUPREME COURT HAS THE NERVE TO GIVE CUSTODY TO THE KID'S GRANDMOTHER BECAUSE HE'D EXPERIENCE "SOCIAL CONDEMNATION" BY LIVING WITH HIS LESBIAN PARENTS. TALK ABOUT A FUCKING **CIRCULAR ARGUMENT!**

97

their brilliant careers

216

©1995 BY ALISON BECHDEL

GINGER! GET YOUR NOSE OUTTA THAT BOOK! I'M TAKING YOU TO DINNER!

LOIS! GET DRESSED! WE'RE GOING TO LA LENTILLE D'OR AND I'M TREATING! I GOT THE JOB!

FOREVER BARBIE

WAY TO GO, GIRL!

HURRY UP AND GET READY! JUNE'S GONNA MEET US THERE. CAN YOU BELIEVE IT? I'M THE SHELTER **DIRECTOR**!

CONGRATULATIONS! SO HOW'S IT FEEL TO BE AN ADMINISTRATOR?

SHE'S PROBABLY GONNA START MAKING US FILL OUT REQUISITIONS WHEN WE NEED TO BORROW A TAMPON.

YOU MUST BE GETTING A HEFTY RAISE IF YOU CAN AFFORD THE LENTILLE D'OR.

CAN I GET THE PORTOBELLO MUSHROOMS FLAMBÉ AND THE SMOKED ATLANTIC SEAWEED?

Over the dessert course...

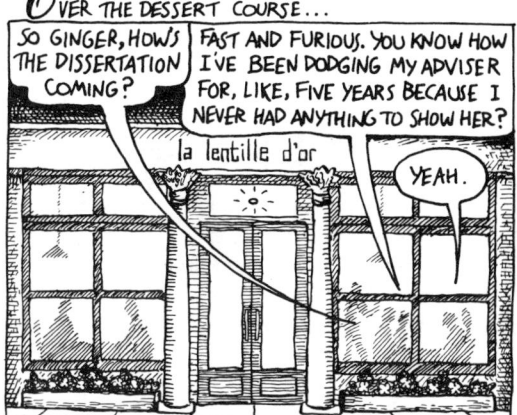

SO GINGER, HOW'S THE DISSERTATION COMING?

FAST AND FURIOUS. YOU KNOW HOW I'VE BEEN DODGING MY ADVISER FOR, LIKE, FIVE YEARS BECAUSE I NEVER HAD ANYTHING TO SHOW HER?

la lentille d'or

YEAH.

WELL, YESTERDAY I SAW **HER** DUCK BEHIND A TREE AS I CROSSED THE CAMPUS. SHE HASN'T READ THE TWO FIFTY-PAGE CHAPTERS I DUMPED ON HER DESK LAST MONTH.

LOIS, WHAT'S WRONG? YOU HAVEN'T TOUCHED YOUR POMEGRANATE-YAM TART!

I DUNNO. I'M JUST THINKING. YOU GUYS ARE REALLY GOING SOMEWHERE WITH YOUR LIVES, AND I'M HAPPY FOR YOU. BUT WHAT ABOUT ME? I'M DOING THE SAME OLD THING I'VE ALWAYS DONE! I'M IN A **RUT!**

LOIS! YOU'RE REALLY UPSET!

EXCUSE ME A SECOND.

After a decent interval...

MAYBE WE SHOULD SEE IF SHE'S ALL RIGHT.

I'LL GO. IF OUR GORGEOUS WAITRESS COMES BY, GET ME ANOTHER CUP OF TEA.

WAIT. HERE SHE IS.

LOIS, WHAT'S GOING ON? ARE YOU OKAY?

YEAH. WHY? HEY, SPARROW! MAKE SURE YOU GIVE OUR WAITRESS A BIG TIP. SHE'S TAKING ME OUT TO SOME CLUBS LATER.

JEEZ, I WOULDN'T MIND BEING IN A RUT LIKE YOURS, LOIS.

I THINK WE MISUNDERSTOOD HER, DARLING. SHE MEANT SHE WAS "IN RUT."

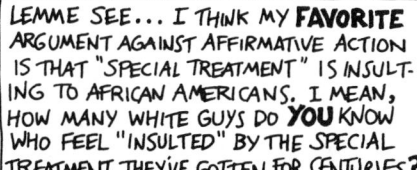

101

another Saturday night

218

THANKS FOR DOING THIS, MO. TONI AND I REALLY NEED TO GET A BREAK.

WHERE **ARE** THOSE TWO?

WHAT TWO?

UH... I FORGOT TO TELL YOU. HARRIET AND ELLEN ARE GOING OUT WITH US.

YOU'RE DOUBLE DATING WITH MY EX AND HER LOVER, THE HUMAN DYNAMO? WELL DON'T **I** FEEL LIKE THE PATHETIC MAIDEN AUNT!

BZZT!

HERE THEY ARE.

HI, GIRLS.

HI! EXCUSE MY SUIT. I HAD TO GO RIGHT FROM A VICTORY FUND RECEPTION TO A MEETING OF THE WOMEN I'M GOING TO BEIJING WITH.

YOU'RE GOING TO THE U.N. CONFERENCE ON WOMEN? HOW EXCITING!

HI, MO. HI, RAFAEL!

NICE TO SEE YOU, MO. ARE YOU THE BABYSITTER?

NO. I'M THE FRENCH TUTOR.

C'MON, LET'S GO! IF WE DON'T LEAVE THIS SECOND, WE'LL MISS THE BEGINNING! I **HATE** THAT!

BYE-BYE! BE GOOD.

DO I HAVE A CHOICE?

WAAAH!

Later that evening...

THALIA
THE BRIDGES OF MADISON COUNTY
7 & 9:30

I WONDER IF WOMEN ARE HAVING MORE AFFAIRS SINCE THIS MOVIE?

WHY SHOULD THEY? THE ULTIMATE MESSAGE IS TO STAY ON THE FARM AND BE A MARTYR.

YEAH, BUT STILL...THE AUDIENCE REALLY WANTED HER TO GO OFF WITH CLINT EASTWOOD. DIDN'T YOU?

CAFE

I DUNNO. I FELL ASLEEP IN THE MIDDLE. WHY D'YOU CARE? THINKING OF LEAVING CLARICE AND RAFFI FOR A STRAY PHOTOJOURNALIST?

UM... NO. BUT I AM KIND OF... UH..ATTRACTED TO SOMEONE. GOD! I ACTUALLY SAID IT! I'M NERVOUS, HARRIET! I NEVER FELT LIKE THIS BEFORE!

TONI, ARE YOU SERIOUS? IT'S GLORIA, ISN'T IT? HAVE YOU TOLD HER? DOES CLARICE KNOW?

CLARICE, D'YOU EVER WONDER IF YOU'RE IN THE RIGHT RELATIONSHIP? LIKE, MAYBE THERE'S SOME MYSTERIOUS STRANGER OUT THERE WHO'S GONNA COME ALONG AND CHANGE YOUR LIFE?

I KNOW TONI'S THE RIGHT ONE FOR ME. BUT I STILL FANTASIZE. DOESN'T EVERYONE CARRY AROUND A MYSTERIOUS STRANGER IN THEIR HEAD?

MAYBE. BUT..UH... WHAT DO YOU DO WHEN THEY SHOW UP IN YOUR BED?

ELLEN! WHAT ARE YOU SAYING? NO, DON'T TELL ME! OH, MAN! DOES HARRIET KNOW?

Meanwhile, mo has a few questions too.

IS THIS EERILY REMINISCENT OF TENTH GRADE, OR WHAT?

WILL I EVER HAVE A LIFE?

ARE MY FRIENDS THAT MUCH MORE STABLE AND MATURE THAN I AM?

the power of speech

219

©1995 BY ALISON BECHDEL

After a most interesting double date, our doting couples find themselves alone at last.

I JUST CAN'T GET OVER WHAT TONI TOLD ME TONIGHT!

WHAT DID YOU AND ELLEN TALK ABOUT ON THE WAY TO THE CAR?

IT'S SO WEIRD TO THINK OF HER BEING ATTRACTED TO SOMEONE ELSE. I MEAN, IN FOURTEEN YEARS WITH CLARICE SHE'S NEVER EVEN **NOTICED** ANOTHER WOMAN!

I HOPE SHE DOESN'T DO ANYTHING STUPID! I'VE SEEN SO MANY DYKES LEAVE GOOD RELATIONSHIPS WHEN THINGS GOT TOUGH, JUST TO CHASE SOME MYSTERIOUS STRANGER.

KOFF!

THEY ALWAYS THINK THE NEW BABE IS THE "RIGHT" ONE, AS IF THEY'VE FOUND THE HOLY GRAIL.

UM...HARRIET? THERE'S SOMETHING I'VE BEEN MEANING TO TELL YOU...

ELLEN'S HAVING AN **AFFAIR?!** CLARICE, HOW COULD YOU WAIT AN HOUR TO TELL ME **THAT?** WHO WITH?!

ONE OF THE WOMEN SHE'S GOING TO THE BEIJING CONFERENCE WITH. ALL THOSE PASSIONATE POLITICAL DISCUSSIONS, I GUESS.

DOES HARRIET KNOW?

NO! CAN YOU BELIEVE IT? I MEAN, IF YOU'RE GONNA KEEP A SECRET FROM YOUR PARTNER, AT **LEAST** HAVE THE DECENCY NOT TO DRAG YOUR FRIENDS INTO IT!

KISS MY TUSH

MOMAZONS

fallin' in and out of love

(220)

© 1995 BY ALISON BECHDEL

CAN YOU CLOSE UP TONIGHT, THEA? I'M NOT COMING BACK AFTER THE DEMO.

I'M TAKING HER ON A PIC-NIC BY THE LAKE.

WOW! THAT SOUNDS GREAT!

HAVE A NICE TIME! AT THE PICNIC, I MEAN. I HOPE YOU DON'T GET ARREST-ED. UH...YOU KNOW, AT THE DEMO.

A PICNIC! GOD, JEZANNA'S BEEN POSITIVELY **MELLOW** SINCE AUDREY CAME ALONG.

YEAH. YESTERDAY I ASKED HER FOR A HUNDRED BUCKS TO PUBLICIZE THE NEXT "MADWIMMIN READ" EVENT, AND SHE SAID, "ARE YOU SURE THAT'S ENOUGH?"

HI! IS THIS WHERE I SIGN UP FOR THE POETRY SLAM?

HARRIET! HI! UH... YOU WRITE POETRY NOW?

JUST KIDDING. I'M STILL THE SAME OLD PHILIS-TINE I ALWAYS WAS. WHO WAS THAT GORGEOUS WOMAN I JUST SAW JEZANNA WITH?

THAT'S HER NEW FLAME, AUDREY. SHE'S AN ONCOLOGY NURSE. THEY MET WHEN JEZ'S MOM WAS IN THE HOSPITAL.

INTENSE. THEY LOOK SO HAPPY TOGETHER.

HARRIET, HOW ARE YOU DOING? I JUST HEARD ABOUT YOU AND ELLEN.

106

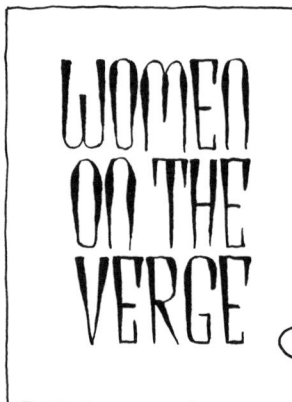

WHILE RAFAEL AND STELLA RECHARGE...

TONI, D'YOU MIND IF I TURN THE RINGER OFF ON YOUR PHONE? SOME-TIMES IT WAKES STELLA.

NO, GO AHEAD. IF ANYONE CALLS, WE'LL HEAR THEM WHEN THE MACHINE PICKS UP.

221

© 1995 BY ALISON BECHDEL

SO. HAVE YOU HAD THE BIG COMING OUT TALK WITH YOUR FOLKS YET?

NO. I CAN'T TELL THEM WHEN CLARICE AND I ARE GETTING ALONG SO BADLY. I REALLY NEED HER TO BE THERE FOR ME WHEN THEY FLIP OUT.

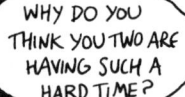

WHY DO YOU THINK YOU TWO ARE HAVING SUCH A HARD TIME?

OH, I DON'T KNOW, GLORIA. MAYBE SHE FEELS JEALOUS OF HAVING TO SHARE ME WITH RAFFI...

...OR MAYBE SHE'S JEALOUS OF YOU.

ME?

WELL, WE DO SPEND A LOT OF TIME TO-GETHER. SHE'S MADE A COUPLE OF REMARKS.

SO HAS ANA. SHE ACTUALLY ASKED ME IF... IF WE WERE SLEEPING TOGETHER.

SLEEPING TOGETHER? WHAT DO THEY THINK WE DO ALL DAY?! WITH TWO TODDLERS, WE'RE LUCKY IF WE MANAGE **LUNCH!**

I KNOW. IT'S KINDA FUNNY.

UM... I WON'T SAY I HAVEN'T THOUGHT ABOUT IT, THOUGH.

REALLY?

OH, GOD! I'M SORRY! FORGET I SAID THAT!

I'VE THOUGHT ABOUT IT TOO. I DON'T KNOW WHY CLARICE DOESN'T TREAT YOU BETTER. YOU'RE SO SWEET AND SO BEAUTIFUL.

OH, NO.

TONI, WE CAN'T!

I KNOW. WE CAN'T.

≥ CLIK! ≤ HI. WE CAN'T COME TO THE PHONE RIGHT NOW, SO LEAVE A MESSAGE! ≥BEEEP!≤

ANTONIA! ESTA ES TU MADRE! I AM VERY UPSET! I WAS JUST BABYSITTING AT YOUR COUSIN CARMEN'S, AND FOUND A STRANGE LETTER YOU WROTE HER ABOUT RAFAEL AND YOUR...YOUR FRIEND. YOU SAY YOU ARE "**UNA FAMILIA LESBIANA**". ¡I AM SICK! ¡I CAN'T SPEAK TO YOU! ¡CALL ME **IMMEDIATAMENTE!**

I KNOW I KNOW THAT. COULD YOU FLESH IT OUT A LITTLE FOR FUTURE GENERATIONS?

WELL, IT WAS THE USUAL SORT OF THING...

SIGH

WE MET IN A WOMEN'S STUDIES CLASS. THEN ONE NIGHT, AFTER GOING TO A CAMPUS DISCUSSION GROUP CALLED " EXPLORING OUR LESBIAN SIDE," WE DID.

JOAN ARMATRADING

I AM NOT IN LOVE... BUT I'M OPEN TO PERSUASION...

WE HAD ONE REALLY NICE SEMESTER TOGETHER, AND BLEW OFF ALL OUR CLASSES EXCEPT " DIALECTICAL REFLECTIONS ON THE SECOND SEX."

WALLFLOWER ORDER

DANCE TROUPE

QUIT IT! THEY'LL TOSS US OUT IF WE BOMB THIS TOO.

WOMEN, CHURCH, AND STATE

M&Ms

DREAM OF A COMMON LANGUAGE

OUR BODIES OUR SELVES

TIP O' THE NIB TO JUDE'S KATZ

113

BUT EVENTUALLY, SHE STARTED TO CRITICIZE ME ALL THE TIME.

D'YOU WANNA TABLE WITH ME TOMORROW AGAINST THE HUMAN LIFE AMENDMENT?

YOU DON'T THINK I'M ACTIVE ENOUGH, DO YOU?

I DIDN'T VOTE IN THE 1980 ELECTION, AND THE NEXT DAY SHE LEFT ME FOR TANYA. LIKE AS IF REAGAN WAS MY FAULT!

AAAAUGH!!

POST-ELECTION PRIMAL SCREAM ON THE GREEN, 3PM

WE DIDN'T SPEAK TO EACH OTHER FOR A YEAR AFTER THAT. BY THEN WE'D BOTH GRADUATED, AND I WAS INVOLVED WITH BEATRICE BUELL.

BEATRICE **BUELL**? THAT WHITE WOMAN WHO DOES SHAMANIC DRUMMING RITUALS FOR RICH SUBURBANITES?

YEAH, WELL. THAT WAS **AFTER** SHE WENT INTO RECOVERY. WHEN I WAS WITH HER, SHE WAS STILL A BIG POLITICO. I LEARNED A **LOT** FROM HER.

YOU CAN BE PART OF THE PROBLEM, OR YOU CAN BE PART OF THE SOLUTION! IT'S LIKE, THE PERSONAL IS POLITICAL!

♪ LEANIN' ON THE PARKIN' METER, HUMPIN' ON THE PARKIN' METER... ♪

DID WE SMOKE ALL THAT HASH?

ANYHOW, BEATRICE WAS WORKING ON THE SECOND WOMEN'S PENTAGON ACTION THAT FALL. I WAS SO INTIMIDATED BY HER ACTIVIST PALS.

YEAH, SUZETTE WAS IN MY AFFINITY GROUP LAST YEAR, BUT SHE LEFT WHEN RENÉE JOINED.

AFFINITY GROUP?! WHAT'S THAT, SOME KIND OF FLOATING **ORGY**?

WOMEN RETURN TO THE PENTAGON

NOV. 15 & 16

OL' BEA HAD A SURPRISE FOR ME AS WE BOARDED THE BUS TO WASHINGTON.

I THINK WE SHOULD EACH BE ON OUR OWN THIS WEEKEND. COUPLE DYNAMICS ARE SO EXCLUSIVE. I WANT TO STAY OPEN TO ALL THE OTHER WOMEN.

8100

GOD! I WOULDN'T BE TWENTY-ONE AGAIN FOR ANYTHING! WHY DO PEOPLE ROMANTICIZE THEIR YOUTH? I WAS STONED AND CONFUSED AND INSECURE AND IN A BAD RELATIONSHIP! WHAT A MISERABLE TIME OF MY LIFE!

LUCKILY, CLARICE'S GIRLFRIEND DITCHED **HER** FOR THE WEEKEND, TOO. WE SAT TOGETHER AND MADE UP.

I HAVE DREAMED ON THIS MOUNTAIN SINCE FIRST I WAS MY MOTHER'S DAUGH-TER

WHEN THE BUS DROPPED US AT THE WASHINGTON COLISEUM, I WAS STUNNED. THE PLACE WAS ASWARM WITH EARNEST, UNTAMED AMAZONS, AND I HAD A CRUSH ON ALL OF THEM AT ONCE. EVERYONE EXCEPT ME SEEMED TO KNOW WHAT WAS GOING ON. I WAS IMMEDIATELY GRIPPED WITH EXCRUCIATING CRAMPS.

I WAS IN AGONY. I FOUND A SPOT WHERE I WOULDN'T GET TRAMPLED, AND CURLED UP ON THE FLOOR.

HEY, ARE YOU OKAY?

UM... YEAH, I'M FINE.

MESSAGES

LOIS, WAIT UP! THIS WOMAN LOOKS SICK!

IT'S JUST CRAMPS. I'M OKAY.

D'YOU WANT A JOINT?

YOU'RE FEVERISH. IT COULD BE TOXIC SHOCK. D'YOU HAVE A TAMPON IN?

NO, A MENSTRUAL SPONGE.

COME ON. YOU'VE GOT TO GET IT OUT. **NOW.**

UNNH! TOXIC SHOCK? D'YOU THINK?

UPS-A-DAISY.

118

THANKS, YOU TWO. :PUFF: THAT WAS A REAL MENSTRUAL HUT KIND OF EXPERIENCE. WOMEN ARE SO WONDERFUL! CAN YOU IMAGINE IF WE RAN THE WORLD?! NO MORE NEUTRON BOMBS OR RACISM OR FEMININE HYGIENE SPRAY!

EXACTLY! WHAT'S SO INCREDIBLE ABOUT THIS ACTION IS THAT IT SHOWS HOW, LIKE, NUCLEAR WEAPONS AND PORNOGRAPHY AND THE LACK OF AFFORDABLE DAYCARE ARE ALL CONNECTED!

HEY, SPEAKING OF WHICH, I'M MISSING THE ANTI-PORNOGRAPHY NETWORKING. I GOTTA GO.

ANTI-PORNOGRAPHY?

YOU DIDN'T KNOW ABOUT LOIS'S ANTI-PORN PERIOD? I GUESS SHE DOESN'T TALK ABOUT IT MUCH.

CLIK!

I GUESS NOT. JEEZ, WE USED UP ALL MY TAPE. THAT'S ALL WE CAN DO FOR NOW.

GOOD. THIS IS DEPRESSING ME. WHERE DID THAT FERVOR AND OPTIMISM GO? I HAVEN'T SAID WOMEN ARE WONDERFUL SINCE MARGARET THATCHER INVADED THE FALKLANDS.

BUT AFTER THE GLOW FADED, SHE STARTED DRIVING ME NUTS.

THE WHITE GUILT FINALLY PUSHED ME OVER THE EDGE.

SO I LEFT HER FOR TANYA. OUT OF THE FRYING PAN, INTO THE FIRE.

I SOMEHOW STAYED WITH HER FOR A YEAR. TILL AROUND THE TIME OF THE SECOND WOMEN'S PENTAGON ACTION. I REMEMBER THE BUS RIDE THERE...

LOOK. OUR GIRL-FRIENDS ARE BACK THERE BLOCKING CONSENSUS ABOUT SOMETHING.

HEY, D'YOU KNOW THE WOMAN SITTING IN FRONT OF ME?

I'VE SEEN HER AROUND. NAME'S TONI. SHE'S AN ACCOUNTANT OR SOME-THING WEIRD LIKE THAT.

IS THAT HER GIRLFRIEND?

I DON'T THINK SO. I HEARD TONI JUST BROKE UP WITH THE BASS PLAYER FOR THE REVOLTING HAGS.

HUH. Y'KNOW WHAT? I'M GONNA MARRY HER.

GROSS ME OUT, CLARICE! HOW PATRIARCHAL CAN YOU GET?

SHHH! WHAT ARE THEY TALKING ABOUT?

...AND RITA HAD THIS AMAZINGLY LONG TONGUE, WHICH SHE KNEW HOW TO **USE**.

DID I EVER TELL YOU HOW LAUREN WOULD CRACK HER KNUCKLES INSIDE ME?

WHEN WE ARRIVED IN D.C., I GOT MY BIG BREAK...

HEY! EXCUSE ME...YOU DROPPED THIS. YOUR BACKPACK IS OPEN

I SPENT THE REST OF THE WEEKEND WITH TONI. TANYA DIDN'T SEEM TO NOTICE.

NO MORE APARTHEID! NO MORE GENOCIDE!

I COULD FEEL AN ELECTRIC CHARGE SURGING THROUGH THE FABRIC TONI AND I HELD BETWEEN US AS WE ENCIRCLED THE PENTAGON.

I FELT A LITTLE GUILTY ON THE TRIP HOME, THINKING OF TANYA IN JAIL... BUT IT PASSED.

A MONTH LATER, TONI AND I HAD OUR FIRST DATE.

UH... I BETTER BE GOING.

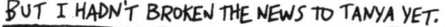

BUT I HADN'T BROKEN THE NEWS TO TANYA YET.

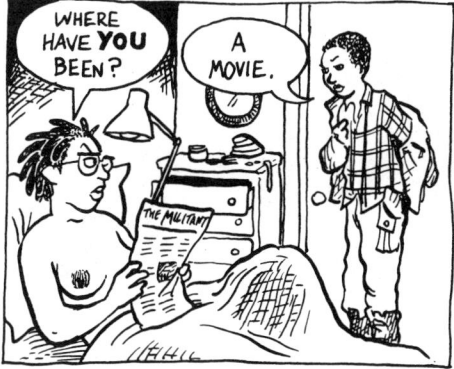

WHERE HAVE **YOU** BEEN?

A MOVIE.

THE MILITANT

BZZZT!

OH, JEEZ! THAT MUST BE TONI! IT'S LATE -- I'VE GOTTA GET TO MY MEETING.

LEMON ADE

HI! STILL AT IT?

MUM MUM!

HI, SPORT.

GOTTA RUN, BABE. HAVE I EVER MENTIONED THAT THOU ART FINER THAN THE EVENING AIR, CLAD IN THE BEAUTY OF A THOUSAND STARS?

NOT LATELY.

IF IT WEREN'T FOR ANA, I DON'T KNOW IF
I EVER WOULD'VE HOOKED UP WITH CLARICE.

DO IT, GIRL! OR I'LL
GO TELL HER WHAT YOU
SAID ABOUT LICKING
COOL WHIP FROM EVERY
SQUARE INCH OF HER
FIRM, LUSCIOUS
BODY!

ALL
RIGHT,
ALL RIGHT!
I'LL TRY
YOUR STUPID
TRICK!

THERE! NOW
QUICK, SLING IT
ONTO YOUR BACK!

HEY, UH...THIS
BANDANA FELL OUT
OF YOUR PACK.

OH, JEEZ. I'M ALWAYS
LEAVING IT UNZIPPED. HEY,
DIDN'T I MEET YOU AT A
POETRY READING?

I'D NEVER BEEN TO AN ALL-WOMEN PROTEST
BEFORE. THERE WAS A REALLY POWERFUL,
HEALING ENERGY TO IT, AS IF WE ACTUALLY
COULD MAKE A DIFFERENCE.

ON THE RIDE HOME, I KNEW I WAS FALLING IN LOVE WITH CLARICE.

A KID? I NEVER REALLY THOUGHT ABOUT IT. I GUESS I'D LIKE ONE. BUT NOT TILL AFTER LAW SCHOOL, OF COURSE.

CLANG! CRASH ding!

WHOOPS! DID THAT BIG LID FALL ON PUMPKIN'S LITTLE FINGER?

SHRIEEK! WAAHAAHAAH

SO THEN WHAT HAPPENED? WHAT ABOUT TANYA?

UH-OH. I'VE GOTTA FEED HIM, GINGER. WANNA HAVE SOMETHING WITH US?

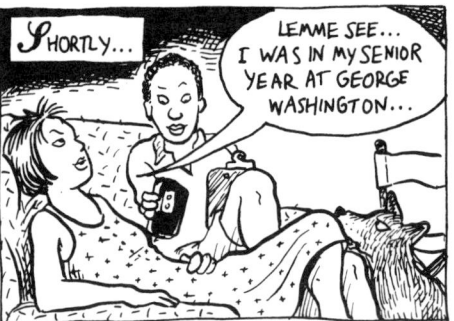

My boyfriend lived off-campus in a kind of collective. Some of the women in his house really intrigued me.

I DIDN'T THINK I WAS A LESBIAN, BUT RALPH WAS SURE STARTING TO GET ON MY NERVES.

THE WEEKEND OF THE PENTAGON ACTION, WE OPENED OUR HOUSE TO WOMEN WHO NEEDED A PLACE TO STAY.

LOIS BEGGED TO DIFFER, AND BY THE NEXT MORNING, I WAS INCLINED TO AGREE WITH HER.

I COULDN'T SEPARATE MY EXCITEMENT ABOUT LOIS FROM MY EXCITEMENT ABOUT THE ACTION. IT WAS SO INTENSE TO CONFRONT THAT MONUMENT OF DEATH AND GREED WITH ALL THOSE WOMEN.

OH! AND WE BOTH MET MO FOR THE FIRST TIME THAT WEEKEND! SHE DIDN'T SEEM QUITE AS MOVED BY IT ALL AS I WAS.

LOIS AND I STAYED IN TOUCH AFTER SHE LEFT. I WAS CONVINCED SHE WAS THE LOVE OF MY LIFE.

AFTER GRADUATION, I MOVED HERE TO BE WITH HER, LIKE WE'D PLANNED. BUT LOIS HAD CHANGED.

I REALLY MEANT IT WHEN I TOLD SPARROW I WAS IN LOVE WITH HER. THE PENTAGON ACTION WAS SUCH A BUZZ.

BUT THERE WAS SO MUCH GOING ON BACK HERE! I'D DROPPED OUT OF SCHOOL BY THEN, BUT I WAS READING EVERYTHING I COULD GET MY HANDS ON.

I'D BEEN REALLY ACTIVE WITH FURIOUS WOMEN AVENGING PORNOGRAPHY FOR THE PAST YEAR...

BUT SUDDENLY, I WAS REALLY CONFUSED.

ADMITTING SOME OF THE THINGS THAT TURNED ME ON WAS LIKE COMING OUT ALL OVER AGAIN.

BY THE TIME SPARROW ARRIVED, I WAS HAVING WAY TOO MUCH FUN TO SETTLE DOWN.

AND IT SOON BECAME CLEAR THAT WE WERE WILDLY INCOMPATIBLE ANYWAY...

I'D JUST BROKEN UP WITH... WHO WAS IT? BETSY, I GUESS. THIS PLACE SOUNDED PERFECT.

AND THE WOMAN WAS SO NICE!

BUT ON MOVING DAY...

BUT **LOOK** AT ME! I'VE BECOME A **GOOD CITIZEN**, FORKING OVER MY TAXES TO SUBSIDIZE STAR WARS AND MASSIVE CORPORATIONS, SO THEY CAN ANNIHILATE THE FEW **SHREDS** OF HUMAN DIGNITY LEFT ON THE PLANET! I EVEN GET **CABLE** NOW!
OH, GET OVER YOURSELF. MAYBE WE DIDN'T SMASH PATRIARCHY. BUT WE'RE ALL CHIPPING AWAY AT THINGS THAT NEED TO CHANGE. IT JUST TAKES LONGER THAN WE THOUGHT IT WOULD.
IF YOU THINK WE'RE NOT MAKING ANY PROGRESS, CHECK OUT THE INTERVIEWS WITH DYKES WHO WERE OUT IN THE **FIFTIES** THAT GINGER GOT AT THE ARCHIVES.
EXACTLY! Y'KNOW, THESE TAPES I'M MAKING ARE GONNA BE SUCH A VALUABLE RESOURCE IN ANOTHER FORTY YEARS. MAYBE I OUGHTA EXPAND THE SCOPE OF THE PROJECT A BIT AND INCLUDE ALL OUR EX-LOVERS.
UH-OH.

142.

Firebrand Books is an award-winning feminist and lesbian publishing house celebrating its tenth anniversary year. We are committed to producing quality work in a wide variety of genres by ethnically and racially diverse authors.

A free catalog is available on request from Firebrand Books, 141 The Commons, Ithaca, New York 14850, (607) 272-0000.